Africa

BACKGROUND FOR TODAY

by Roy MacGregor-Hastie

Illustrated with maps and photographs

By elucidating the past, the author hopes the reader will have a better understanding of what is happening today in this vast and baffling continent.

The mass of material covers the colonization, exploration, slave trade, development of resources, and rebellions that marked the various phases of Africa's history.

Beginning with the first colonies that were established by European countries, the author explains why this colonization took place, what those who emigrated to Africa found there, how they lived, and their relationship with the natives.

The book also includes the movement for freedom, outlining some of the complex problems now confronting the independent states.

In clear, simple prose, a wide range of information is presented on a subject about which too much cannot be written. The maps and chronological tables increase the value of this volume for the classroom, as well as for the general reader.

Africa

BACKGROUND FOR TODAY

BY

ROY MacGREGOR-HASTIE

ILLUSTRATED WITH PHOTOGRAPHS

CRITERION BOOKS

NEW YORK

By the same author:
POPE JOHN XXIII
POPE PAUL VI
THE THRONE OF PETER

FOR DR. A. J. BERGSMA

An Intext Publisher

Printed in the United States of America

22156

CONTENTS

ILLUSTRATIONS

I

EVEN TODAY, FOR MANY PEOPLE, AFRICA IS THE CONTINENT of hot, wet jungles, inhabited by Negroes. The continent is considered politically exciting because, for the first time in history, its inhabitants now rule themselves in well-organized states.

None of these popular beliefs about Africa is true.

Africa is certainly hotter than northern Europe, Russia or Canada, but it is not uniformly hot. In the Sahara Desert, of course, it is very hot indeed, but the Sahara occupies less than a third of the continent. In the rest of Africa, there has never been a temperature recorded as high as the temperature on some summer days in New York or Adelaide. The north and southeast African .coasts have climates similar to those of the French or Italian Rivieras, and are popular holiday resorts for Europeans. In eastern central Africa, there are large areas of land, high above sea level, where warm clothes are essential for much of the year.

Again, *some* of Africa is tropical jungle with a high rainfall, but this is less than one-sixth of the continent. There is much more rain forest in southeast Asia 'and in some parts of South America than there is on the so-called Dark Continent. Africa south of the Sahara Desert consists almost entirely of dry grasslands, much like the open prairies of North America and as sparsely dotted with trees. Rainfall is much less than in most of Europe and America, and tends to come during one season of the year only. Even the Sahara Desert was once dry grassland, on which cattle grazed. It is more rocky than sandy—the soil has disappeared from the Sahara over many centuries, from causes still debated by historians.

Nor is Africa populated exclusively by Negroes. North of the Sahara Desert there are very few Negroes. The people of Egypt, Libya, Algeria, Tunisia, Morocco and part of Ethiopia are largely Arabs. They are Muslims, speak Arabic (and often French) and feel as foreign in "Black Africa" as do Europeans. There are Europeans all over Africa, many from families settled on the continent for generations. South of the River Zambezi there are over three million Europeans, mostly of British or Dutch origin, and they all consider themselves to be Africans.

Negroes were not even the earliest inhabitants of the African continent. When the Negroes came on the scene, between 6000 and 4000 B.C., there were already pygmies in the forests and bushmen on the dry grasslands of south and east Africa. Nobody quite knows where the Negroes came from, though they were almost certainly the first inhabitants of the Sahara Desert. Probably they evolved from the race which first inhabited northeast Africa, more or less where Ethiopia is now.

North of the Sahara, a different race predominated, and though there was contact for trade between the races, the great desert kept them quite separate as civilizations.

Many people are surprised to learn that there were Negro civilizations before the arrival of the European. Yet a century before Christ, the people of the Niger Valley were using iron implements to clear the forest and work the land. Descendants of these people moved slowly south with their knowledge of agriculture, reaching South Africa about A.D. 1500.

The Sahara Desert seems to have become uninhabitable at about the time of Christ. Trade then began between the Negro peoples of the Niger Valley and the Berber-Arab peoples of north and northeast Africa. The Negroes needed salt, and offered slaves and gold in exchange. Wealthy kingdoms were soon established in the Niger Valley, at first under Berber domination, and formed the Empire of Ghana. About the year 770, the Berbers were ousted, and a Negro dynasty ruled the empire. The present state of Ghana, which does not occupy the same territory, was named after this ancient empire.

The Ghanaian empire, which flourished for more than five centuries, was highly organized. To the south, in what is now the Republic of Guinea, gold was mined, the finest in the known world, by tribes who were not really under the emperor's control. Leaders of the tribes would come to the banks of the Niger and build a small shelter, under which they would place the gold nuggets they had to trade. One of the emperor's court officials would wave acknowledgement, at which the tribesmen would disappear. The gold was then inspected and a rough calculation of its worth was made. Next to the gold shelter another shelter would be built, under which the Ghanaians would pile salt and leather goods, iron tools and ornaments. The Ghanaians would recross the river to their own side and wait for the tribesmen to reappear. If they were satisfied with the exchange for their gold, they would take away the salt and other items, and leave the gold to be collected by the Ghanaians.

Trade with the Berbers to the north was done more simply, in markets set up for the purpose in Ghanaian cities. Salt would be bought with the gold and the empire would pocket a profit for acting as middleman. The Ghanaian emperor also maintained an army to protect his trading partners and seems to have maintained a court as civilized as any in Europe. There were painters and scholars at the court, which was much admired by visiting Arabs who have left accounts of their stay as guests of the emperor.

An early eleventh-century emperor became famous as a man of peace, in an era better known for its warlike leaders. He was horrified to hear of the invasion of the north by "uncivilized" Arabs from the Near East, and told his Berber friends they could safely migrate to the southwest of his empire and settle along the Senegal River. Unfortunately for the emperor, the Senegalese Berbers came under the influence of a fanatical Muslim leader, Ibn Yasin, who preached holy war against all the infidels, including the Ghanaians. At first many of the Berbers took sides with the emperor against Ibn Yasin, pointing out that they had survived as a tribe only because of Ghanaian generosity, but in the end a holy war was declared.

Defeated in battle, the Ghanaian emperor was forced to abandon his capital and flee to the north of what is now Nigeria, together with his family and his court. Those of his subjects who remained at home were either slaughtered or forced to become Muslims. Where the Ghanaian Empire had been, a new Empire of the Mali was established, and this became one of the wealthiest and most fanatical states of the Muslim world.

The Mali emperors, who ruled from the Atlantic coast to the Niger River unchallenged for four centuries, were the first Negroid statesmen to come into contact with Europeans.

During the eleventh and twelfth centuries, successive emperors filled the treasury and built a splendid city at Timbuktu. It was a city certainly larger than London at that time, and it stood at the heart of a web of trade routes wider than most others in the western world. Timbuktu was famous for its palaces, for its worked gold and fine cloths, though the Arabs who have described it may have exaggerated the degree of luxury in which the emperors lived. After a journey across the Sahara Desert, any comfort must have seemed luxurious. Nevertheless, it is known that by the end of the thirteenth century there were many brick and stone buildings in the city, one group of them housing a Muslim university second only to that on the Nile as a seat of learning.

Early in the fourteenth century, some Venetians trading in Cairo were amazed to see a prince enter the Egyptian city whose wealth and royal presence rivaled their own Doges'. When they asked who the man was, they were told that it was Alhaji Mansa Musa, Emperor of Mali from 1307 to 1332, on his way home from a pilgrimage to Mecca. The Venetians were intensely curious, and over the next twenty years a score or more of them visited Timbuktu, by far the most important city on the continent. Venetian glass and silverware in some quantity has been found during excavations there.

Inevitably, the wealth of Mali attracted the attention of would-be conquerors inside and outside Africa. The

A view of Timbuktu from a drawing made in 1828 by Rene Caillie, who, disguised as an Arab, was the first European to penetrate the city *Photo: Radio Times Hulton Picture Library*

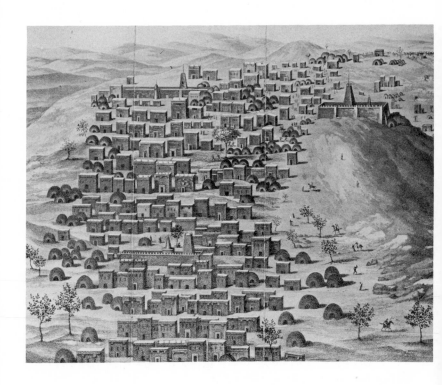

Muslim leader of the Negro Songhai people rebelled against the Mali emperors to whom he owed allegiance, and in the same year that Columbus crossed the Atlantic, the Songhai established a new dynasty. The Askia kings of Songhai extended Mali rule even further, to the west. However, they were not all great kings and emperors, and they surrendered to a Moroccan invading army in 1591. The Askia family were the last great independent rulers of West Africa. By the time the Moroccans had made themselves comfortable in Timbuktu, the first Europeans, Portuguese explorers, had set up trading posts along the Guinea coast, and the era of white exploitation of the continent had begun.

Negroes did not appear in East Africa in any numbers until about A.D. 600—in spite of the supposition that their ancestors had lived in and migrated from this part of the continent. All the so-called Bantu, or Bantu-speaking Negroes, trace their origin to tribes which once lived in West Africa, and the dates of the "Great Journeys" recorded in their folklore allow one to wonder if they had something to do with the rise of Ghana. Certainly the first Bantu in East Africa were a warlike people, whose journeys across Africa had toughened and helped them to organize themselves. The primitive Stone Age peoples living alongside the Great Lakes were soon overwhelmed. Bushmen fled south. Pygmies remained, more or less as hereditary slaves to the new Negro invaders.

The first Bantu state to become settled, rich and powerful was Buganda. The Bugandans tilled the land around Lake Victoria with iron implements; their kings were adventurous, and sent ambassadors to the north and east to trade. Cattle were brought down from the Upper Nile and flourished on the lakeshore pastures.

Buganda had the first civil service in Africa. Government was honest and efficient. Chiefs were appointed to administer new territories which were conquered or asked to join Buganda; taxes were levied and paid over to the central administration. It is easy to see how just and efficient this administration was when history records its continuance, with power unabated, until 1869, the year the first Europeans arrived on the scene.

Other Bantu tribes did not stop at the Great Lakes but moved south to what is now the Republic of South Africa, or farther east to the coast. The South African Bantu became settled farmers and, in the area which is now Rhodesia, seem to have established a wealthy and powerful state. The ruins of the stone city of Zimbabwe show that up to the end of the fifteenth century an advanced civilization flourished there.

Those Bantu who reached the East African coast in the eleventh century were the first to find a higher degree of civilization than the various Bantu civilizations they had left behind. The whole coast line from Malindi to Sofala was dotted with settlements. There were mosques and palaces on offshore islands, and an astonishing mixture of races. Arabs from the Arabian peninsular port of Muscat had been trading along the coast for five hundred years, driven to do business at sea by the unfriendly desert behind Muscat. They had been joined in the ninth century by refugees from Persia, then conquered by the Turks, and the coastal cities had a definite Persian feeling. Other Arabs built up a valuable trade with India and China and, inevitably, Indians and Chinese settled along the East African coast to protect their trading interests. To add to the confusion, the coastal settlements were known collectively as Zinj, which means "Ethiopia," though Ethiopia never formed part of Zinj.

The unfortunate Bantu found that they could not over-whelm the civilizations of the city states of Zinj. What happened was that the Arabs and Persians consolidated their position as the leisured rulers of the states, leaving the physical trading to the Indians. The Bantu became the workers and, worse, they also found themselves shipped to India and China as slaves. Gold supplemented the slave trade, and in return the merchants in the Far East sent cloth and spices. Trade with China. expanded steadily, even when wars in India and the Arabian penin-sula isolated Zinj from the north. Contact with China might have resulted in a large Chinese settlement along the coast had not a fifteenth-century emperor decided to destroy all Chinese vessels capable of ocean sailing "to preserve the purity" of the Celestial Empire.

One contribution of Zinj to African culture was the evolution of a common language understood by Arabs, Bantu and Indians alike. The words were a mixture of Bantu and Arabic, with a few phrases in Hindi, and the whole was written in the Arabic script and called Swahili. It is still the lingua franca of East Africa. Vasco da Gama (1460-1524), the Portuguese explorer, was the first Euro-pean to land at a Zinj port. He thought that the spoken Swahili was the language of the lost Christian kingdom of Prester John, which was supposed to have existed about three hundred years earlier in the mountains of Ethiopia.

By the time that Europeans discovered East and West Africa in the fifteenth century, the native Negro and his Berber, Arab, Indian and Chinese partners had had considerable experience with social, political and economic organization. The Ghanaians, Mali and Bantu had built cities of stone, with paved roads and simple but efficient sanitation. They had strict laws for keeping wells clean, and when there was sufficient water, organized public bathing. Their governments had civil services, systems of taxation and public spending for education. Probably as high a percentage of Ghanaian courtiers could read and write as courtiers of the English and French capitals of the Middle Ages.

2

THE EUROPEANS WHO ARRIVED IN AFRICA IN THE FIFTEENTH
century did not set out deliberately to colonize the continent; they were not empire-builders, nor did they come
looking for slaves. The Portuguese, the first Europeans to
land on Black African territory in about 1452, were on
their way to India. They were anxious to find new
sources of spices for the large market at home. The
Venetians had a monopoly of trade with the Far East,
dealing with merchants who brought goods overland, and
the Portuguese wanted to break that monopoly. Prince
Henry the Navigator of Portugal (1394-1460), who had a
passionate interest in sailing, encouraged seamen to find
a route for "caravans by water," and they thought of
Africa at first as simply a place to take on food and water
and to make repairs to their ships.

Interest in Africa itself grew when several ships' captains came home with the news that there was plenty of
gold to be had on the Guinea coast. The Fanti tribes
along the coast were friendly, and wanted to trade. They
needed cloth and salt, and could be made more friendly
with gifts of polished metal and mirrors, beads and bright

pictures. The first trinket or souvenir industry seems to have been created to make trade with West Africa easier.

It is not certain just when the first slaves were bought by the Portuguese and taken back with them. What is certain is that they were few in number and bought only for their "novelty" value, to work as servants in the private houses of rich Portuguese noblemen. It remained fashionable to have Negro boy pages for two hundred years, and the pages were usually very well treated. The Elmina Treaty, signed between the Fanti tribal leaders and the Portuguese in 1482, makes no mention of slaves at all. Whatever slave trade existed at the time was organized by Negroes themselves. The Hausa tribes, in particular, captured slaves from weaker tribes and sent them overland to serve Muslim sovereigns. The Turks were especially good customers, as were some Hausa rulers themselves.

The trickle of pageboys to Portugal became a slave trade when the Spanish and Portuguese began to open up South America as a huge "farm for Europe." The first explorers of South and Central America were attracted by the gold, as were the first explorers of the African coast, but it soon became obvious that the soil and the forests were even more promising than the gold mines. Europe had been badly farmed for thousands of years and was becoming less fertile. Chemical fertilizers were unknown and agricultural implements were primitive. South America, on the other hand, was a vast and empty subcontinent whose few inhabitants had never even scratched the soil in many regions. One acre of the best land in Brazil could feed as many people as five acres in Portugal. There was only one snag to farming in South America—the heat. Portuguese peasants could not work in that heat all the year round. Anyway, there were too few peasants in Europe to work the enormous plantations cleared in Portuguese and Spanish South America. Negro slaves were needed badly, and as the Spanish and Portuguese could pay higher prices than other customers, they soon had a grisly near-monopoly of the trade.

It would be wrong to think that the Church, which had divided South America between Spain and Portugal, closed its eyes to the horrors of the slave trade and did nothing about it. Missionaries accompanied the first traders to Western Africa, as well as the first settlers in South America. These missionaries were excited at the prospect of converting millions of pagans to Christianity. In Africa, they were also excited at the prospect of stopping the spread of Islam, as they had stopped it in Europe. Muslims had slaves, because Islam taught that there was nothing wrong with "protecting" those who could not look after themselves. Christian missionaries, in the beginning, were determined to stamp out both Islam and the slave trade.

Unfortunately for these missionaries, merchants and traders in West Africa were already making fortunes shipping slaves across the Atlantic. These traders argued that there had always been slavery in Africa, so they were not guilty of any new abuse of human rights. They were also ready to promise that all the slaves would be converted to Christianity, so they would be spiritually better off. In any event, the traders were not prepared to allow missionaries to interfere.

Prevented from working in West Africa, where Islam and slavery were well rooted, the missionaries of the late fifteenth century decided to start work in the Congo. There was slavery there, but few Muslims or white

businessmen. In 1483, a group of missionaries was successful in converting the king of the Manicongo, who was
baptized and renamed King John. But King John, though
he was grateful for missionary advice on how to farm
more efficiently and organize his state more profitably,
was not enthusiastic about abolishing slavery and giving
his people "equal rights before God and man." His son
was a more sincere convert, and in 1502 the missionaries
left King John's capital of Mbanza and moved 125 miles
to the coast with the young man. The king's son set up his
own government on the coast, and built many fine
churches. He abolished slavery by decree and even began
to discuss an education program for his people.

The missionaries were unlucky again, notwithstanding
this promising start. In 1503, King John died and his
son had to return to Mbanza (which he renamed Sao
Salvador) to be crowned as King Alfonso. No sooner had
he settled down in Sao Salvador than his slave-free coastal
settlement was captured by friends of the Portuguese who
had settled on Sao Thome Island and needed slaves for
their sugar plantations. Both King Alfonso and members
of the missionary order protested to the Portuguese king,
Manuel I, but he had lost all interest in Africa and was con-
centrating on the development of new settlements in India.
The black king did not despair, even when most of his
missionary friends were recalled. He went on raising fine
buildings, among them the first cathedral in Africa, and his
own son became a priest and later Bishop of the Congo.

It would be pleasant to record that King Alfonso and his
son triumphed over the greed of Negroes and Europeans
dealing in slaves, and certainly Portuguese handbooks
continued to list the Manicongo as a Christian ally until
the end of the nineteenth century. But the truth is that,

abandoned by the Portuguese kings and missions, the Manicongo royal family gradually retreated from Christianity and became slave traders, too.

By the end of the sixteenth century, the whole of the African coast from the Canary Islands to modern Angola had become a well-organized source of supply for slaves. The South and Central American plantations became more and more profitable, and needed more and more slaves. The Fanti tribes along the West African coast could no longer supply slaves in sufficient numbers and some Europeans began to explore the interior and capture the inhabitants for themselves. Fortresses and prisons were built, and direct rule from Portugal established over all the settlements. The profits from the slave trade reached astronomical proportions and the Portuguese became almost dependent on the exchange of "black gold" for "yellow gold," of slaves for the precious metal.

The size of the profits soon began to attract traders and ships' captains from other countries. The Dutch, like the Portuguese interested in India, established their own revictualing stations along the West African coast and soon began to take on as many slaves as casks of water. Not only did the Dutch rival the Portuguese as buyers of slaves; they also managed to compete successfully in the South American markets as sellers to Portuguese and Spanish settlers, using their own Dutch Guiana as a base. The success of the Dutch aroused the interest of the British and French. Until the end of the seventeenth century, British and French shipowners concentrated, too, on supplying slaves to Spanish and Portuguese markets in South and Central America. Thereafter they had their own colonies in the West Indies and North America which took as many slaves as they could buy or capture.

The British, French and Dutch seldom invaded the interior in search of slaves. Only the Spanish and Portuguese had depots far from the coast. The French made contracts with the chiefs of tribes in present-day Senegal and the Gambia. The British took over the forts the Portuguese had built along the Gold Coast and built trading stations in what is now western Nigeria. The Yoruba, Fanti and Senegalese guaranteed to supply an agreed number of slaves every year and, in turn, made contracts with the chiefs of the Hausa and the Ashanti in the interior. The coastal tribes supplied cloth and salt in exchange for the slaves, and lived off the profits they made as middlemen. The Dutch tried to deal direct with the Ashanti, which infuriated the Fanti along the Gold Coast, who began to give the British and French the best slaves at a discount for honorable and friendly behavior.

It is important to remember that although European traders made fortunes out of the slave trade, none of them benefited quite as much as the Negro kings of the Ashanti, Benin and Dahomey tribes. Before the arrival of Europeans, the Ashanti tribes had been farmers, living for the most part in peace to the southeast of the Mali and the southwest of the Hausa empires. They profited by the breaking-up of these empires to capture slaves of their own to work their lands. It was a short step from that to going into business with the Fanti, who seemed to have a limitless demand for slaves and similarly limitless supply of cloth, salt and white men's weapons. Chief Anokye brought all the Ashanti tribes together into one kingdom and made them warriors. Wars were waged throughout the hinterland of the Gold Coast and captives sold to the Fanti. As a result of other wars, the Ashanti were able to win the monopoly of supplying salt to the tribes living south of the Sahara in old Ghana and Mali, and were able to demand payment in slaves.

The kingdoms of Dahomey and New Benin were also founded on the slave trade. Benin had been a flourishing, peaceful state famous for the work of its artists in bronze. With the arrival of the Portuguese on the coast and on Sao Thome Island, a new market was created for food, and later for slaves. The Portuguese made agreements with the rulers of Benin, guaranteeing to take a thousand slaves a year. Benin warriors suddenly found themselves called upon to go "hunting" along the coast of what is now western Nigeria, but the tribes they hoped to capture and sell into slavery were much more skillful in war than they were. They told their Portuguese partners that they had to have white men's weapons if they were to fulfill their part of the agreement. Most Europeans were not very enthusiastic about giving firearms and powder to Negroes, for fear that the weapons would be used against them, and the Portuguese were no exception. They reluctantly handed over to the Benin a small supply of firearms. However, they had not reckoned with the skill of Benin metalworkers, who within a comparatively short time produced hundreds of "homemade" pistols and muskets. With the aid of these arms, Benin became a powerful military state, waging war regularly once a year, and living off the booty and slaves that were captured.

Naturally enough, the Yoruba tribes who lived to the north, inland from Benin, were not pleased to have such a warlike neighbor where previously there had been a peaceful state. The Yoruba organized their own defence, and trained their cousins the Dahomeans who populated the coast to the west. It was a profitable partnership.

The Yoruba continued to cultivate the land, taking over fields on the Benin frontier that their neighbors had abandoned—"a warrior does not work the land." The Dahomeans specialized in soldiering and a tight state organization. The Yoruba did the feeding, the Dahomeans the fighting, and by the middle of the seventeenth century they had reduced Benin to ruin, taking over the right to supply the slave markets. Dahomey became probably the greatest warrior nation in the history of West Africa, the first to divide its army into corps of specialists—a transport command, a supply corps, even a corps of women soldiers who acted as guards for the captured slaves.

Anthropologists have tried to calculate the precise number of slaves sold to Europeans in the four hundred years that the slave trade flourished. There are no reliable records of the numbers bought, and no records at all of the number who died on the voyage across the Atlantic, battened down in the hold. But it seems likely that about ten million Negroes were shipped out of West African ports, two million of them dying en route. Before Europeans came to Africa, about two million slaves had been sold through Arabs and Berbers to the north. These are horrible figures to contemplate.

By the middle of the eighteenth century a movement had begun in Great Britain to abolish this "despicable commerce." It was the anti-slavery movement, rather than the slave trade itself, which gave birth to the great European empires in Africa.

The first murmurings against the slave trade were heard in Spain, in the first years of the eighteenth century. A Jesuit priest pointed out that though Spain considered the slave trade unlawful, and forbade Spanish ships to

ABOVE: Map from a book published in 1888

BELOW: An African slave market of 1870.
Photo: Radio Times Hulton Picture Library

take part in it, nothing was done to prevent Spanish citizens in America from owning slaves. The priest said that condemnation of slavery was just hypocrisy, unless something was done to free those enslaved.

It was the Quakers who emancipated the first slaves, in their settlement in Pennsylvania. The Society of Friends, to give the Quakers their full title, discussed the whole question in 1726 and 1727, and decided that it was anti-Christian to preach that one man could own another. English Quakers and English Methodists realized that the religious argument would not really convince men who had thousands of pounds invested in slaves and slave-run plantations, so they formed the Anti-Slavery Society. The object of the Society, formed in 1765, was to petition the British government to declare slave-owning and slave trading illegal. It took seven years for the petition to be considered by the Lord Chief Justice, Lord Mansfield (1705-1793), and his judgment was not altogether satisfactory. Lord Mansfield said, in fact, that while he was in sympathy with the Anti-Slavery Society, he could only declare slavery illegal inside the United Kingdom. He could make no ruling for the colonies, and in any event, the American colonies where slavery was rife were in revolt. Nevertheless, a start had been made, and the Society found itself with hundreds of slaves who had been living in England, and thousands more who had fled from the American colonies to Canada. A new future could be made for them. They could be taught to enjoy their new-found freedom.

Fifteen years after their emancipation, the first Negroes were returned to Africa. Both Quakers and Methodists believed that this was the right thing to do. Freed slaves could not stay on where they might embarrass their former masters, and it was believed that they would be happier in the jungle. The anti-slavers forgot that many of the unfortunate Negroes had never seen Africa, and of those that had, many probably came from parts of Africa other than the coast of Sierra Leone where the first resettlement was made in 1787.

Moreover, the natives of Sierra Leone were not pleased to see these freed slaves returned as settlers. It was impossible to buy land for farming, because native law did not recognize the purchase or sale of land. Rents were fixed so high that the members of the Slave Resettlement Board found that their freed friends needed larger and larger subsidies to keep them from starvation. One secretary to the Board reported that former slaves were being forced to take jobs with slave traders in order to earn enough money to stay alive. In desperation, the Board appealed to the British government, which agreed to take over the settlement as a Crown Colony and make itself responsible for the new arrivals. When the Colonial Office in London began its direct rule of Sierra Leone in 1808, this marked the beginning of Empire in Africa.

In 1816, the second freed-slave settlement was made in Africa. The American Colonization Society was given a charter in that year to find a place for former slaves who were becoming a problem in the cities of the United States. The Society was not particularly humane in its outlook and was supported financially by many southern slave-owners who wanted to remove "discontented" Negroes from the American scene and leave only those who at least pretended to be content with their lot as slaves. The humanitarians were confined to the northern members of the Society who believed that their proteges would cruise up and down the Congo singing "in the language which records the Constitution, laws and history of America, hymns of praise to the Common Parent of mankind."

In 1821, some land was bought to the south of the Sierra Leone settlement and named Monrovia, after President Monroe. As more land was bought it was known as Monserrado County, and Monrovia was considered the capital. Farther south, more land was bought and named Bassa County, and another section, settled in 1825, was called Maryland. The total American Negro population of the settlements was about 22,000.

The American Colonization Society did everything possible to give Liberia, as the settlements came to be known, a good and efficient government. Independent from 1847, the state had a model constitution drafted by Harvard University's Law School and all the mechanics of democratic government. Unfortunately, the settlers were not particularly democratic. Although they had been slaves themselves, they soon became involved in slave trading and treated the inland tribes very badly. Many members of the Society were bitterly disappointed. The southern plantation owners who had supported the Society for their own reasons claimed that the Liberian experiment proved that Negroes were not fit to rule themselves.

After 1815, the determination of British governments to stamp out slavery everywhere in the world made them take a steadily increasing interest in West Africa. No one wanted to claim colonies in the part of Africa known as "the white man's grave." Living conditions for British officials were thought to be impossible, and the experience with Sierra Leone had discouraged those who felt it their duty to protect weaker tribes against the stronger. Nevertheless, British merchants had made treaties with African tribes, notably the Fanti, and British governments felt obliged to respect those treaties. The Fanti were protected by British troops against the Ashanti, for example, but at the end of the Ashanti war of 1825-1828, the British government of the day withdrew its troops and left West Africa to the merchants and the Africans themselves.

Until the second half of the nineteenth century, there were, strictly speaking, no colonies in West Africa. Sierra Leone and Liberia went their own way, without much help or interference from Britain or America. Along the coast British, French, Danish, Dutch and Portuguese forts protected private interests. Apart from the isolated British or French explorer, the tribes inland seldom saw a European. Peace was restored by a Fulani Muslim, Uthman dan Fodio, to tribes made bankrupt by the ending of the slave trade. He conquered a large part of what is now Nigeria. Ahmadu, who died in 1898, restored peace similarly to the tribes of modern Senegal, and his followers ruled over the whole of the grasslands on the southern edge of the Sahara.

It was left to men whose driving force was mainly religious to pave the way for European settlement and colonizing of the African continent.

3

*Dutch Boer settlers in South Africa; Boer
religious fanaticism; French Calvinist settlers;
foundation of Graaff-Reinet Republic;
British troops occupy Cape and Graaff-Reinet
Republic; the Great Trek; the Boer republics;
nineteenth-century missionary explorers;
gradual European occupation and control of
Africa; Berlin Conference 1884*

THE FIRST CHRISTIAN COMMUNITIES IN AFRICA WERE IN THE north. The Coptic Church was established in Egypt and modern Ethiopia in about A.D. 180. In the northwest, more or less orthodox communities were established, acknowledging the primacy of Rome. By the end of the eleventh century, however, Muslims had overrun all these communities except that of the Copts in Ethiopia.

As we have seen, Catholic missionaries followed traders to West and Central Africa, but their converts were small in number and were defenceless when Portugal lost, interest in the continent during the seventeenth and eighteenth centuries.

The men who came to Africa "with the Bible in their hands," and stayed, are still the rulers of the south. They were Dutchmen, and though in 1647 their ancestors intended to set up only a staging post for India-bound ships, they proved to be the most stubborn European settlers on the continent.

Before the arrival of the Dutch, the part of South Africa south of the present Vaal River was inhabited only by primitive Bushmen and Hottentots. The Hottentots were slightly more advanced, owning and developing several breeds of cattle, but they did not live in any sort of organized society. To the north of the Vaal River, Sothi and Ngoni armies were a threat to Hottentots living on the open plains. The Sothi and Ngoni were the first of the descendants of the Bantu migrants who had settled in East Africa to start a new migration south.

The first Dutch settlers arrived at the Cape of Good Hope in April, 1652. The "Cape Colony" was to be dependent on the East India Company in the Dutch East Indies and ruled from there. A local governor, Jan van Riebeeck (1618-1677), was appointed at the Cape ; he was supposed to make the settlement self-sufficient and produce a surplus of food which could be supplied to ships on their way from the Netherlands to what is now Indonesia.

Jan van Riebeeck had a difficult task. His peasant settlers, called Boers, did not treat him with the respect he thought he deserved. They were not patriotic, because the Netherlands had not been independent from Spain for very long, and loyalties at home were to the village and the Church rather than to a crown or flag. The Boers also disliked van Riebeeck in his capacity as representative of the East India Company. Many of them had hoped to go direct to the East Indies and make their fortunes there, and they resented being dropped off at the Cape of Good Hope to make a living on less fertile land with few of the trimmings of civilization. Whenever van Riebeeck tried to raise taxes, many of the Boers would just pile their belongings into a cart and "trek" off into the interior to find new land outside the Company's official territory.

In 1657, Negro slaves from West Africa and Malays from the East Indies were brought to the Cape to work the land abandoned by the Boers. They were to try to grow crops more suitable to the climate and soil than the European fruit and vegetables which had failed. Difficult relationships between the Boers and the slaves, and between the Boers and the Hottentots with whom they traded, made it impossible for van Riebeeck to rule a "tidy" colony. There was, in fact, little central government. Capetown was a small settlement, under some control. From time to time, the Boers would drive cattle down from the interior to Capetown; the cattle would be traded for guns, ammunition and seed. Van Riebeeck needed the cattle if he was to supply ships with fresh meat, so he was forced to buy. He would then raise money by taxing the purchase of meat and various supplies.

In the interior the Boers ruled themselves. Heads of families chose the magistrates who would dispense justice, and the officers to lead their local defence forces. The Boers came to own their land after holding it on lease for five years. Once the land was theirs, they did as they pleased on it. Had Van Riebeeck sent a party of soldiers north from Capetown to enforce his own conception of law and order, his soldiers would have been fired upon by local "commandos." The only law the Boers knew was their own interpretation of the Bible, and the Bible was the only book in which they placed a limitless faith. Adherence to the tenets laid down in the Bible would bring salvation. Since there was no other way to salvation, it followed that it was not available to anybody who did not agree with the Boers' interpretation of the High Dutch Bible that was kept in every trekker home. Catholics, Negroes, Muslims, even other Protestants were damned. Negroes and Muslims were particularly unfortunate because there was no hope of salvation for them. Catholics and other Protes-

tants might be saved if they abandoned their own inter-
pretations of the Old Testament and of Christ's teachings
in favor of Boer Christianity.

The religious fanaticism of the Boers did not necessarily
make them cruel to Negroes or other colored people.
Many Boers in the early days lived with Negro or other
colored women, and treated these "temporary wives" and
their children (Griquas, or people of mixed European and
Hottentot blood), with the same severity and justice they
were to use when they formed a permanent family by
marrying a Dutch girl sent out from the Netherlands. Anybody who sinned against the Bible or against the authority
of the head of a family was whipped, regardless of his color.

In 1686, four thousand Huguenots fled from religious
persecution in France and came to South Africa via the
Netherlands. They were Calvinist Protestants, like the
Boers, and readily merged with the earlier settlers. They
brought with them women who made good wives, and a
French appreciation of culture which helped to make the
lives of the original peasants a little softer and more
elegant. The Cape governor hoped that many of the
Huguenots would remain in Capetown, but they preferred life on the farms inland. The Cape authorities were
eventually forced to invite an association of German
merchants to settle in the city and run its expanding
commerce. By the end of the eighteenth century, the Cape
interior was populated by an independent community of
Boers and Huguenots, living according to the teachings of
the Bible. The original settlement, on the other hand,
which was responsible to the Dutch East India Company,
was an uncertain mixture of races and religions. The Cape
was stagnant; the interior was full of vigor, expanding in
numbers and ambition.

In 1794, under the influence of the French Revolution, a Boer republic was proclaimed by Dutch-Huguenot settlers five hundred miles from the Cape. The Graaff-Reinet Republic, it was said, would guarantee liberty, equality and fraternity to its population of four thousand. The real reason for the declaration of independence was the Boers' belief that the Cape administration could not protect them from Xosa cattle-stealers or from the Zulus, a new wave of migrants from the north. In 1795, British troops occupied the Cape to protect Britain's own trade routes to the east against the French, who had conquered the Netherlands. The British administration did not understand the Boers' way of life, and immediately decided to suppress the Graaff-Reinet Republic as a potential pro-French danger to security. In 1799, the Republic was invaded, and the territory brought back, in theory, under the control of the Cape.

If the British had been content with conquest, and a guarantee of protection to the Boers, all might have been well. But there were unpleasant surprises. The London Missionary Society, which was politically very powerful in England, persuaded the government to permit the establishment of a mission station at Graaff-Reinet. In charge of the station they put the Rev. Johannes van der Kemp (1747-1812). To the Boers, van der Kemp was just about the worst choice the Society could have made. Not only was he a Dutchman who had betrayed the faith of his native country and become an Episcopalian, but his personal morals were very doubtful. Van der Kemp increased their distrust by acting as a spy for the Cape administration, informing on farmers who failed to pay their taxes. He took action upon his own beliefs, which were in direct conflict with those of the Boers; after

1807 he tried to enforce the ban on slavery. He also attempted to give Hottentots equal rights in land ownership, and even to recruit them to a colored police force.

For the Boers, justice, land ownership and government were matters which could only be settled by what their Bible dictated. A man who was not "saved" could not rule, administer justice, or own land in the same district as the "saved" Boers. Van der Kemp was obviously a devil promoting evil. When he sent Hottentot policemen to arrest Boer farmers for non-payment of taxes, riots broke out which were only suppressed by hanging the ringleaders.

The British governor of the Cape, Lord Somerset (1768-1831), took the riots and the hangings in his stride. He was more concerned with the threat to the security of the colony by Zulu and other warring tribes on its northern frontiers. He believed that the colony would only grow strong when English settlers outnumbered the troublesome Boers, who could then be taught to respect the British way of life. Lord Somerset abolished Roman-Dutch law and replaced it with British law. He made English the official language of the colony, and was horrified when two-thirds of the old settlers took their children away from school rather than have them taught in English. All this was bad enough, but when he put the Dutch Reformed Church under his supervision and appointed Scots ministers to preach in English, it became obvious to the Boers that they could not protect their Bible and their way of life while they remained under British rule.

In 1835, one hundred and fifty families of Boer-Huguenots began the Great Trek away from "godless" British rule, and began, too, what came to be known as "the scramble for Africa."

Preparations for the Great Trek which began in 1835. One of a series of fifteen embroidered panels hanging in the Voortrekker Monument in Pretoria. *Photo: courtesy South African Embassy*

The Cape governor at the time, Sir Benjamin D'Urban (1777-1849), tried to stop the Trek by persuading the government in London to pass the Cape of Good Hope Punishment Act (1835), which provided that settlers would remain subject to the colony's laws even if they left "temporarily." The Boers' leader, Piet Retief (1780-1838), took no notice of the Act, and left himself in 1837 with a further two thousand trekkers. His attitude was that the Cape governor had shown himself unable to protect the Boers from the Negroes, so could scarcely enforce the law beyond the colony's frontiers. There was also an interesting attempt by the new Committee of the London Missionary Society to persuade the Boers that they would not be overwhelmed by Negro free farmers. John Philip (1775-1851), who succeeded van der Kemp, suggested that the races could be kept apart in different areas, and in this way would not come into conflict. But apartheid was not to attract the Boers as a solution for another hundred years. In 1835, they felt that it was too late for compromise.

After strenuous journeys across inhospitable country, the trekkers who survived massacre by hostile natives managed to establish two republics, Potchefstroom in the northwest and Natal in the northeast of South Africa. Potchefstroom was ruled by A. H. Potgieter (1792-1852), and Natal by A. W. J. Pretorius (1798-1853), who had taken Piet Retief's place as leader of the main body of Boers. From 1838 to 1841 both Potgieter and Pretorius strove to make their new homes prosperous and secure. Pretorius had the easier task. He had the use of the port of Durban, a sure market for cattle and farm produce, and he was able to organize the native Zulus under a single chief, Cetewayo (d. 1884), with whom he made a treaty. Pretorius even created a "Volksraad," or parliament, of twenty-four men elected by heads of families. Potgieter, on the other hand, ruled his republic more or less as a dictator. Conditions in Potchefstroom were much more difficult and the struggle for survival made any notion of democracy absurd. But the Bible, a simple faith, and a determination to survive linked the two republics though their capitals were hundreds of miles apart.

The British government was not pleased at the prospect of success for Pretorius or Potgieter. In 1841 the government declared that it could not recognize any so-called independent republics on Crown territory, claiming that all of South Africa was British. In 1843, Britain declared that Natal was a British colony. As a compromise, the Colonial Office was prepared to offer any farmer, British or Boer, six thousand acres to stay under British rule.

But again, the Boers refused to compromise. They did not want to co-exist with English missionaries, under a government which would make English the official language of Natal. Another trek began, to the north, and three new Boer republics were established—Utrecht, Lydenberg and Zoutpansberg. Pretorius went west and founded the Winburg Republic, but this was suppressed by the British two years later and Pretorius was forced to flee to Potchefstroom.

For eight years the republics beyond the River Vaal lived in an uneasy state of peace, harried by the Bantu and uncertain of the British government's intentions. But the British government had no wish to acquire territories for which it would be responsible. The idea of Empire was still unpopular. It was felt that colonies cost money ; merchants made the profits, but the Crown had the expense of maintaining law and order, and could only do so by raising taxes. In 1852, the Vaal republics were recognized as independent states, and in 1854 the Winburg Republic was revived and given its independence as the Orange Free State. In 1860 the Vaal Republics united to become the Republic of South Africa, better known as Transvaal.

But the Boers' success in dealing with the British did not bring them peace. While there were constant wars with the Bantu, these were not too serious. The serious issue was the series of internal quarrels in the Church. The Dutch Reformed Church had been freed from state control by the British Cape Administration in 1843, and divided into three independent synods—one for the Cape, one for the Transvaal and one for the Orange Free State. But even the independent synods were suspected of being under British, that is Scots, influence, and the Transvaal established its own church, the Hervoormde Kerk. A third, even purer and more puritannical church was established in 1859. Known as the Dopper Church, it declared that it was "ungodly" to speak English, say the world was round or suggest that a Negro had a soul.

Half a century of Boer "amateur" religious activity resulted in an extension of European occupation of Africa greater than that of three centuries of slave trading.

The various missionary societies, the "professionals," were alarmed at the thought of Boer expansion. The London Missionary Society held that all three Boer churches preached heresy and would make the conversion of the pagan Bantu difficult in the future. And so a series of explorations by missionaries began which had two consequences. A part of Africa was Christianized, and popular interest in Africa was aroused by the heroic exploits of some of these missionaries. This popular interest in Africa was soon reflected in the decision by many European governments to move into Africa, to export the European way of life and share it with the African.

Probably the most famous of all the missionary explorers was David Livingstone (1813-1873). A Scots doctor, he first came to know the Africa of the Boers when he served in a mission on the frontier of the Orange Free State. He was distressed by much of the Boers' religious teaching, especially the doctrine that the Negro could never achieve salvation because he was inferior. Dr. Livingstone explored most of what is now Rhodesia and Zambia, and he also got to know Angola and Mozambique well. He wrote books and papers about his travels, which became bestsellers in Europe and America. H. M. Stanley (1841-1904), a Welshman who had emigrated to the United States, joined Livingstone in Africa and was himself responsible for opening up most of the Congo.

In the wake of the missionaries came the soldiers and the politicians. Africans used to say: "Once we had the land, and Europeans had the Bible. Then came the missionaries and soon we had the Bible and Europeans had our land." The last decades of the nineteenth century saw the map of Africa colored by European states. Certainly the Africans themselves were not consulted as to where the lines should be drawn.

Livingstone's fellow explorer, Stanley, was probably responsible for more of these lines than any other man. He explored much of East Africa, and on a journey in 1875, reported to the Church Missionary Society in London that the Kabaka of Buganda would be glad of Christian help against the Muslims north of Uganda. Both the Anglican Church Missionary Society and the Catholic Church sent missionaries. The Anglican missionaries asked for British protection and this was granted, mainly because British traders at Zanzibar needed protection, too, against the Arabs. Catholic missionaries were anxious for the protection of a Catholic power in the same area. Portugal, willing to give this protection, claimed that the whole of East and Central Africa was hers, and that the British had no right to nibble at it from the north or the Boers from the south. Catholic missionaries in the Congo, their routes mapped for them by Stanley, asked for French and Belgian protection. King Leopold of Belgium (1835-1909) and Napoleon III of France (1808-1873) showed their willingness to increase the French and Belgian presence in the area, in spite of claims by Portugal that the Congo was hers. Napoleon III also expanded France's interests in West Africa, claiming sovereignty over most of the area south of the Sahara. Germany claimed that she protected a large part of South and East Africa.

The British government of the 1870's looked upon the

claims to Africa by other nations with some amusement. They felt that a state could only claim the ownership of another if the state claimed were "effectively occupied." The French, Spanish, Portuguese and Germans could claim what they liked, but were they in "effective occupation?" The British government thought not. There were only thirty-six consuls resident in the whole of Africa in 1880, and most of them were British. Two-thirds of the European and European-officered troops on the continent were either British or French. British trade accounted for seventy per cent of all trade with Africa, and six out of ten African chiefs who had made treaties with a European power had made them with Great Britain.

Nevertheless, the British did not want to claim all of Africa. Disraeli (1804-1881) had encouraged enthusiasm for the idea of Empire, but nobody wanted the high taxes that would be needed in order to build the roads and pay for the troops to control a whole continent. Though Africa seemed to have natural resources, it would be years before this wealth could be taken to Europe. Without the slave trade, there was no easy way to riches. There were rumors of gold and precious stones in South Africa and in some parts of the Gold Coast, and this was all that interested the government in London, although they were prepared to offer protection to missionaries and traders in East Africa on a limited scale.

The German prime minister, Bismarck (1815-1898), realized that quarrels about Africa could lead to a war in Europe. Great Britain was the only country that had successfully carried out an industrial revolution, and Bismarck was anxious for peace so that Germany could catch up. This argument for peace seemed sensible to the

French government, too. Neither Spain nor Portugal was ready for a European war, and the government of the U.S.A. felt that it would not be in the interest of Liberia if the continent were ravaged by troops.

Bismarck called a conference of the "African powers" in Berlin in November 1884. The United States and Great Britain dominated the conference. The United States was concerned with the safety of the Liberian experiment, although many delegates pointed out that the Liberian government and the Portuguese were the only ones not taking strong action against slavery. The United States' spokesman was also concerned with prohibiting the use of alcohol by Africans in general. Great Britain's representative stated again his government's belief that "effective occupation and management" was the only criterion by which a country could claim colonies. British missionaries made sure that this representative would insist on the protection of Anglican missions in East and West Africa.

The 1884-5 Conference decided that Africa should become an appendix to Europe. West Africa was divided between Britain and France, with tiny territorial concessions granted to Spain. East Africa became British, as did South Africa, both with German colonies recognized as "legal." Portugal was conceded Angola and Mozambique, since the occupation of the Portuguese in South and Central Africa could not be disputed. The Congo was divided between France and Belgium. Liberia was recognized as "inviolable," and alcohol was prohibited in the Congo and in East Africa. No one at the Conference devoted much time to the Boers, whose religious fanaticism and desire for freedom had been responsible for the annexation of an entire continent.

4

French domination of Algeria, Morocco and Tunisia; the Mahgreb; spread of French influence in North Africa; Libya; Italian control of Libya; Egypt; early history; independence in 1805; British Protectorate in 1884; the Sudan

AT THE 1884 BERLIN CONFERENCE, THERE WAS LITTLE talk of European states' rights in North Africa. This was for the very good reason that, apart from the British presence in Egypt to protect the Suez Canal, the whole of North Africa was thought to be a "natural preserve" for France. The Turks, it was true, occupied Libya, and there were Spanish and Italian traders in some number in Tunis and Morocco, but nobody seriously disputed French supremacy.

Algeria had been annexed by France in 1839. There had been close trading relations between Algeria and France since the sixteenth century and the first French consulate had been established in 1581. As the Turks lost their hold on this distant province of their Empire, French traders moved in, and by the end of the second decade of the nineteenth century there were hundreds of French settlers in and around Algiers. In 1844, exploration of the Sahara began, and effective occupation of the whole territory with its Arab-Berber population.

Algeria was an attractive area for colonizing. It was not too far away from metropolitan France—just across the Mediterranean in fact—and the climate of the northern region was similar to that of southern France. On the northern coastal plain, settlers soon found they could grow grain, grapes, citrus fruits and olives. The hot dry summer and autumn rains allowed the production of cork and dates, and the first geologists to explore the interior suggested that there was lead, copper, zinc and iron in the mountains and who-knew-what under the Sahara.

Neighboring Morocco and Tunisia were equally attractive as potential colonies. The climate of Morocco—situated between the Atlas Mountains and the Atlantic Ocean—was found to be temperate, though hot and dry in the south and east. Three rivers, Moulouya, Sebou and Oum Er Rbib, watered plains and plateaux on which fruit and vegetables grew and livestock grazed. Lead, zinc, cobalt and manganese were found in the mountains. Morocco's wealth and convenience as a "staging post" for Black Africa aroused interest in many European trading capitals and there was a minor war in 1845, which was won by the French.

Tunisia, before it became a French protectorate in 1881, probably had the most contact with Europe. From the first century A.D. until the year 700, it was one of the great early centers of Christianity. Here Saint Cyprian and Saint Augustine lived and worked. The loss of Tunisia to the Muslim invaders was a great loss to western Christian civilization. Spain liberated and occupied Tunisia for forty years, from 1535 to 1575, but the Turks reoccupied the country and held it as a province of the Ottoman Empire. As the Empire began to break up, Tunisia sank deeper and deeper into political and economic chaos; order was finally restored by the French

A house in Tafraout, Morocco, showing the characteristic style of architecture   *Photo: courtesy Moroccan National Tourist Office*

in 1881 under the provisions of the Treaty of Bardo.

At this time, Tunisia was primarily an agricultural country, with grain, olives, wine and some livestock. The French found the climate as agreeable as the better parts of Algeria and Morocco.

Just before the proclamation of the French protectorate in Tunisia, there was a repetition of the earlier minor war won in Morocco by the French in 1845. The newly-united Italian peninsula was governed by men full of nationalism, not all of which had been used up in the struggle for re-unification. There were many Italians in Tunisia in the 1870's, and strong pressure was put on the government in Rome to "make the Italian presence felt" in Africa. But the government was weak, and the infant Italian state unable to challenge France.

By 1884, the whole of the so-called Mahgreb (Tunisia, Algeria and Morocco) was a zone of undisputed French influence. The nearest to France of the Mahgreb countries—Algeria—was fast becoming a settled French colony, and soon there were so many French settlers in Algeria, and Algerian workers in France, that the country was considered a part of France itself.

Historians have offered several explanations for this colonization which was not quite a colonization.

France, during the nineteenth century, was not a particularly stable country. There was a series of revolutions and coups. The monarchy was restored, then deposed. There was a new republican constitution, then the Bonapartes were restored as emperors, then a new republic was instituted. The chaos and confusion led many Frenchmen to believe that a move across the Mediterranean to the comparative peace and quiet of Algeria would enable them to live without strain or interference. Many of the monarchist landowners and peasant supporters of the Bonapartes established plantations and farms in Algeria as a protest against the deposing of their idols. Life in the new "North African France" was easier as well as more peaceful. Taxes were lower and there was a ready supply of servants available among the poor Arab-Berbers. The land was easy to till, and the settlers were soon prosperous. In turn they attracted shopkeepers and professional men from "home." By the time of the outbreak of the First World War, hundreds of thousands of settlers were so firmly rooted in North African soil that they were known as "pieds noirs" (black feet).

French governments during the latter part of the nineteenth and early part of the twentieth centuries approved of the settlement across the narrow sea. It removed politically discontented people from metropolitan France, and put them far enough away so that they could not trouble the unstable republic. Only small French garrisons were needed in the Mahgreb, and the taxes collected, though light, were more than enough to pay for protecting the settlers.

Some visionaries, visiting Algeria and seeing the vast vineyards, believed that the colony and the south of France would become great food and wine-growing areas, serving and served by a completely industrialized northern France. North Africa as a whole would also become the market for French manufactured goods, with certain "preferences" in the way of low customs duties. French industrial and agricultural products would slowly work their way around the Mediterranean, dominating the markets of the area, including the Middle East. The entire Arab world would become "French" in tastes and commercial preferences, and this would offset Britain's influence in the Mediterranean.

Other dreamers thought of Algeria and the rest of the Mahgreb as a "jumping-off point" from which all of West Africa could be conquered, politically and commercially, again rivaling Britain. There were among this second group of dreamers a number of hard-headed businessmen and engineers who believed that France could expand slowly to the south, exploring and exploiting the land as it was opened up. Many mining engineers believed that below the Sahara Desert there were deposits of minerals, and probably oil. Nothing had been taken out of the Sahara since it had become a desert, and there was a variety of minerals in the known part of the Mahgreb. Why could it not become another Texas?

Unfortunately for the dreamers, successive French governments were slow to invest money in North Africa. Most prime ministers in Paris wanted the colonies to be self-supporting, so that metropolitan France would not have to raise taxes for the development of other areas. It was only after World War I that local and imported capital was available in sufficient quantities for a proper exploration of the region, and even then the glowing reports of geologists failed to move the inefficient governments which succeeded each other so rapidly in Paris.

Until shortly before World War II, Tunisia, Algeria and French Morocco (Northern Morocco was given to Spain in 1912, and Tangier made an international zone in 1923) were merely settled, rather than exploited. This did not prevent many settlers from amassing large fortunes and living in great style, but it meant that the everyday lives of the native Arabs and Berbers remained unchanged. Around the original Mahgreb cities, French business and residential quarters were built, soon completely surrounding the native cities or "Casbahs." The two groups did not mix socially; a native Algerian would have been just as horrified if his daughter had told him she wanted to marry a Frenchman, as a Frenchman would have been to hear that his son wanted to marry an Arab girl. The rich Arabs and the wealthy French settlers met from time to time at government functions, but there was no apparent desire to integrate the two communities. The only gestures settlers made to the customs of their new country were to wear lighter clothing and to eat some of the native dishes.

The Roman Catholic Church at first made some effort to convert the peoples of the Mahgreb to Christianity, so that "pieds noirs" and natives would at least have their religion in common. But efforts at conversion met with little success. The peoples of the Mahgreb, notwithstanding their history of early Christianity, were devout Muslims. The rigidity of Catholics and Muslims on the question of intermarriage was partly responsible for the fact that no Franco-Algerian community was ever formed. Many French bachelors who went to Algeria on official business and fell in love with Arab girls were astonished to find that the girls' parents would not hear of their daughters marrying an "infidel" Christian.

After World War I, the Church's mission effort in the Mahgreb lessened. The non-Muslims of Tunisia and Morocco never exceeded five per cent of the population; in Algeria the figure was even smaller. In Tunisia, the number of Jews was larger than that of Christians. The major missionary effort in Africa was made in Black Africa, south of the Sahara.

The colonial history of Libya is somewhat confused,

because nearly every imperial nation seems to have occupied a part of it at some time or another. The coast of Libya was first colonized by the Greeks, about six centuries before Christ, and then conquered by the Romans who penetrated far into the interior. The coastal strip seems to have been wider during the first part of the Roman occupation, from 146 B.C. to A.D. 429, and the oases in the desert interior more numerous. Roman remains have been found in areas quite uninhabitable today. In A.D. 429, the Vandal king Genseric, who ruled from 428 to 477, destroyed the Greco-Roman civilization of Libya. His successors were expelled by the eastern emperors expanding from Constantinople.

In 642, the great wave of Islam swept over Libya, adding a mixture of races to the native Berber, and the country has remained largely Muslim ever since. In 1145 the Norman Dukes of Sicily occupied the principal city, Tripoli, and their successors lost it to the Spaniards in 1510. The Spaniards in their turn were expelled in 1551 by the Turks, who ruled more or less uninterruptedly until 1911.

In 1911, frustrated by the French in Tunisia, Italy invaded Libya, and the following year Turkey renounced all rights in the area. Until 1943, the country was a self-governing colony, advised from Rome.

The Italians, as in Eritrea to the southeast, left the greatest visible mark on Libyan life. Poor peasants who had come from Sicily found the climate similar to their own, and worked hard to make agriculture more efficient. Olive groves were replanted, and the raising of cattle and fishing were properly organized. Roads were built and an attempt was made to irrigate dry lands from the rivers Sofeggin and Megenin. Untidy settlements which had been little more than staging posts for nomads became sizeable towns—among them Misurata and Barce —and the two cities of Tripoli and Benghazi were tidied up by the Italians.

Benito Mussolini (1883-1945), Duce of Italy from 1922-1943, was anxious to settle as many Italians as he could in Libya, so that he could control shipping in the Mediterranean between the Libyan and Sicilian coasts. When he fell out with Britain after his invasion of Ethiopia in 1935, he needed his own Gibraltar to protect supplies for his troops in Ethiopia and Somalia. Libya benefited considerably from Mussolini's military activity—more roads and two airports helped to attract Italian capital to exploit deposits of sulphur and to begin a proper exploration of the interior.

Like Libya, Egypt became a Roman province, though it was not until 31 B.C. that the Battle of Alexandria saw the defeat of the successors to the Macedonian king Alexander the Great (356-323 B.C.), who had conquered the country himself in 332 B.C. Alexander had ruled a country whose civilization extended back some three thousand years. He had tried to preserve whatever was still good and workable in their agricultural methods, as did the Romans who followed him. However, the Muslims who invaded Egypt in A.D. 640 laid waste the once rich country, and during the centuries of Turkish rule the desert made inroads on the fertile valley of the Nile.

As the Turkish (Ottoman) Empire became weaker and more corrupt, Turkish domination of Egypt became less and less effective. Britain and France fought over Egypt during the Napoleonic Wars, without feeling obliged to consult the imperial government in Constantinople, and the Khedive of Egypt, Mehemet Ali (1769-1849), declared the country an autonomous province in 1805. There was no reaction from Constantinople, and by 1820 Mehemet Ali was behaving like an independent sovereign and waging wars (against Buganda) on his own account.

Yet the politically free Egypt could not be truly independent. Agriculture, on which the country's livelihood depended, seemed to have made little progress since the decline of the last pre-Christian dynasty. Irrigation canals had silted up and no improvements had been made in the design of implements since the invading Hittites had brought with them the iron with which to tip ploughshares two thousand years before. The Pyramids, the architectural miracle of the old Egypt, seemed, like the country as a whole, to be sinking into oblivion in the sand.

The leaders of an Egypt only recently freed from Turkish dominance were quite ready to give up some of their independence in return for a method of regaining solvency. British businessmen were the first to take an interest, closely followed by the French. The mills of the textile revolution needed more and more cotton, and the war of 1812 with America had encouraged a search for other supplies for British mills. Good cotton grew in Egypt, and with British capital the plantations were reorganized and expanded. A French project for digging a canal from the Mediterranean "to the Indian Ocean" also intrigued the British government which immediately saw the economic and military advantages of the much shorter sea passage to India. In 1869, the Suez Canal was opened and soon confirmed these advantages. In 1884, because of the difficulties then facing the French government, and a general feeling in France that it would

The opening of the Suez Canal in 1869
Photo: Radio Times Hulton Picture Library

be better to concentrate on the Mahgreb and the Middle East, Britain was able to buy the majority of the shares in the Suez Canal Company and thereafter governed Egypt alone as a protectorate.

One of the political problems facing Britain after the establishment of the protectorate was the revolt of the people of the south, or Sudan, of Egypt. From 1340 to 1820 the Sudan had been independent, a Muslim kingdom known as Fung. In 1820, however, Egypt, with Turkish help, had conquered Fung and ruled it uneasily until 1881. Then a revolt led by Mohammed Ahmed El Mahdi, (1844-1885), ended effective Egyptian rule. It took British troops, with Egyptian help, until 1898 to reconquer the area, which was then named the "Anglo-Egyptian Condominium of the Sudan." A certain amount of local autonomy was still vested in a council in the capital, Khartoum, but for all intents and purposes the

Sudan became again an Egyptian colony. Throughout the period of British rule, efforts were made to make both the north and south self-supporting. Some success was achieved in Egypt proper, and the cities of Cairo and Alexandria flourished as commercial centers for the Middle East. The large Christian population of these cities—nearly sixteen per cent (mostly Copts)—made it easier for the European commercial communities to settle down there. Little was done to reclaim the desert or repair the irrigation canals, however, and the country began to import large quantities of food with the money earned in commerce. The only crop which benefited from any considerable investment of capital was cotton.

The Sudan was more difficult to develop. The north of the Sudan is desert (to the north and northwest of the Nile) or mountainous (east of the Nile), and the southern region—a well-watered, fertile plateau—was both hostile and inaccessible. The Muslims, who make up seventy per cent of the population of the Sudan, were hostile to "infidel" Christian Europeans who came to rule them, and the pagan twenty-four per cent of the population was hostile even to local government. It was found that cotton and all the food grains grew well in the southern region, but the local labor force was unreliable, and fanatical Muslims were always liable to burn the crops.

The French, and to a lesser extent the Italians in Libya, were the only real colonial settlers in North Africa, and the only people to transplant new ideas which helped the north of the continent to develop the traditional strengths of the local economies. The French in Algeria were certainly the only people to become "African," emotionally part of their new home.

Ethiopia; first Christian empire; Italian colonization in the twentieth century; British exploration of East Africa; Lugard, Johnston and the foundation of Nyasaland; Uganda; Christian missionaries in Uganda; religious conflicts; Uganda a British Protectorate; foundation of Kenya; German East Africa ceded to Britain as Tanganyika Territory; exploration of the Congo; King Leopold of Belgium; Belgian exploitation of the Congo

5

THE OLDEST CIVILIZATION IN EAST AND CENTRAL AFRICA is the Ethiopian. Nobody knows quite how old it is, but the ancient Egyptians certainly knew of it and traded with the "Negus Nagasti," the "King of Kings," a title enjoyed by the Ethiopian kings since 300 B.C.

Ethiopia covered what is now Ethiopia and Somalia. A great part of Ethiopia consists of a plateau 8000 feet above sea level, with mountains rising out of it to a height of 14,000 feet. The plateau extends toward the Valley of the Nile where the first contacts with Egyptians were made. In the east there are lowlands extending as far as the Red Sea and Somalia. Life on the almost inaccessible plateau seems to have been agreeable. The climate is temperate and healthy in contrast to the hot and humid coastal lowlands. An aristocracy of cattle raisers seems to have lived on the plateau, and the Negus established himself there, though the first Negus was a king of Eritrea.

There are many legends about the origin of the kings and people of Ethiopia. Some say that the Negus was a descendant of King Solomon, the "Lion of Judah," and that the Ethiopians are the only unconquered tribe of Israel. Whatever the truth may be, they were certainly the first people to be converted to Christianity en masse, and Ethiopia became the first Christian empire, during the first century A.D.

The Muslims who swept across North Africa and down the East African coast in the seventh century seem to have stopped short at the foot of the high mountains. In 1268, the re-established dynasty of "Lions of Judah" counter-attacked Islam and by the time the first Europeans, the Portuguese, reached the country in 1527, the empire was Christian again.

The Portuguese found themselves in something of a dilemma with the Negus. They had made their way to the empire hoping to use it as a base for the conversion of East Africa. The Negus received them politely, but told them that he had no intention of reconciling the National Church with that of Rome. He was all for spreading Christianity—his country had been the only significant outpost of the faith in Africa since the seventh century—but he insisted that his version of the faith was as good as any other. Horrified by his persistence in this heresy, the Portuguese lost interest in him. It was not until 1896 that another European nation, Italy, tried to establish a political presence, tied to a desire for religious conformity, in Ethiopia.

The Italians were prevented from establishing them-selves in Ethiopia until 1935-6, when their military operations left them in command of the whole country.

There were a number of reasons for the Italian victory in 1936. The Ethiopians in general were not enthusiastic about their new Negus, Haile Selassie (1892-   ). Tribal leaders looked with suspicion on his plans for modernizing the country, afraid that they would lose their feudal power. The Church welcomed the Italians because Haile Selassie seemed to be doing nothing to abolish slavery in Ethiopia. Generals De Bono and Graziani were met by church leaders as "liberators." And the peasantry felt that their emperor was more interested in making his mark internationally than in attending to problems of poverty and disease at home.

Italian colonization of Ethiopia was remarkably thorough. In the best Roman tradition, the country's first network of adequate roads was built. The roads were needed for military use, but they helped in the general reorganization of the marketing of agricultural products and in giving a sense of law and order. Italian settlers opened shops and operated the country's first health services, and the peasant farmers who settled there increased the output of maize, wheat, barley, millet, sugar cane and coffee. A ready market for coffee was found in Italy, and it soon rivaled cattle hides as the country's main export.

The men who opened up East Africa, south of Ethiopia, were British. There had been Arab settlements along the coast for centuries, controlled from Zanzibar by the rulers of Zinj, and it was at Zanzibar that the British established a consulate to protect British shipping and discourage the Arab slave trade. However, it was difficult to deal with slavers and to discourage them once they already had the slaves. A thorough exploration of the interior was needed so that the supply of slaves could be stopped at the source.

David Livingstone was the first man to make the necessary exploration in depth in 1856, followed on several occasions by scientists, J. H. Speke (1827-1864), J. A.

Grant (1827-1892) and Sir Richard Burton (1821-1890), searching for the source of the Nile. In 1859, Livingstone founded a mission on the shores of Lake Nyasa. He began to preach the evil of slavery to the tribes, and to suggest to them that there were other forms of commerce just as profitable. He had a small steamer brought up to the lake in sections, convinced that he could use it to prove this last point. But the local Yao tribesmen were difficult to convert. They had given up their farming for the slave trade and they had no desire to go back to working the soil. The mission station itself was always harassed by disease, and after a few years the steamer began to leak irreparably.

It was not until 1873 that a new mission, properly equipped and well situated, was established in Nyasaland. The missionaries worked closely with officials of the African Lakes Company to expand local commerce and to put down slavery. The Company had its own small army, with whose aid it "persuaded" the Arab sheiks to decrease their slaving activity and to keep the peace on the lake. But the Portuguese in Mozambique, over whose territory traders had to pass, were neither friendly nor helpful to the Company. The Portuguese were not inclined to help either a non-Catholic mission or a rival trading company, and it was not until Lord Salisbury, (1830-1903), induced the Portuguese government to give up its claims to duties and transit fees that trade became stable. In 1887 there was another setback when the Arab sheiks broke the truce in protest at the launching of another steamer on Lake Tanganyika. For the next three years there was a real war, paid for by the Company, against the Arabs. The war was only won when the Company engaged an experienced officer on leave from the Far East, Captain

Sir Frederick Lugard (1853-1945)
Photo: Radio Times Hulton Picture Library

Frederick Lugard (1853-1945), to direct the operations of its little army.

In 1889, Lugard went to London to try to persuade the government to take an official interest in the area. His place as the moving spirit in Nyasaland was taken by H. H. Johnston (1858-1927), acting as consul.

Johnston was an active, idealistic humanitarian, who was dedicated to the abolition of what remained of the slave trade and to the spread of Christianity. He believed that he would only win the confidence of the tribes when he showed that Europeans were willing to live and work in Nyasaland alongside the Ngoni, Yao, Tonga and Chewa native tribes. He encouraged settlement, and accompanied new arrivals to the huts of native chiefs, to introduce the neighbors. He drew up deeds for land sold by the chiefs to the settlers, limiting the total land sold to five per cent of all Nyasaland. Johnston did not want it said that Europeans had crowded out the original inhabitants.

Between 1889 and 1891 Johnston talked to most of the chiefs and explained to them the policies of the Company, and the desire of the missionaries to help the natives find "spiritual and physical health" in churches and hospitals. The chiefs made treaties with Johnston, acknowledging Britain's protection, and in 1891 even Portugal recognized Nyasaland's status as a British Protectorate. The British government, however, would only accept responsibility for mission areas, and so Nyasaland lost the area which was later to be known as Northern Rhodesia. The British South Africa Company took over the Lakes Company, and Nyasaland (it received the name officially in 1907) continued its existence as a "pure Christian colony."

The British settlers in Nyasaland soon became accepted

members of the multiracial community. They lived down the legend, circulated by Arab slave traders, that the Africans they sent to England to be trained were really eaten instead by the White Empress and her Court. British capital was invested in the growing of tea and tobacco, and the agriculture-based economy had become prosperous by the beginning of World War I.

Nyasaland quickly became the most Christian colony in Black Africa. Nearly half the population, black and white, was baptized by the turn of the century, and the number of mission schools increased dramatically year by year. It was said that it was easier for an African to get a good education in Nyasaland than anywhere else on the continent.

Johnston's success as an administrator in Nyasaland made him a natural choice as peacemaker in the troubled Uganda, to the north across the waste of German East Africa. Johnston (by this time Sir Harry Johnston) arrived in December 1899.

Uganda had been discovered by J. H. Speke while on a scientific expedition in 1862. He found there the Baganda (or Ganda tribe), whose stable, prosperous nation was called Buganda. It was ruled by a wise king, or Kabaka, who was worried by the extent to which Arab slave traders were penetrating his kingdom. The Baganda aristocracy, which held its land from the Kabaka in return for its responsibility to raise troops for defense and to levy taxes, was being bribed by the slave traders, and it was difficult to dismiss and replace local chiefs each time a case of corruption came to the king's notice. Conditions had worsened by the time Stanley reached Uganda in 1875, and the Kabaka of Buganda, Mutesa, asked if missionaries could be sent to protect the kingdom from slave traders and other Muslims. Mutesa knew that Christian missionaries were morally opposed to slavery, and "professionally" hostile to Islam. He believed that he could neutralize the threats to the security of the Baganda by playing off Christian against Muslim advisers.

Kabaka Mutesa could not have foreseen what in fact happened. His invitation to missionaries was eagerly accepted. The Church Missionary Society in London sent out a group of Anglican teachers, ministers and doctors. French enthusiasts sent Catholic Carmelite White Fathers. Catholic and Protestant missionaries united at first against the Muslims, but within two years were quarreling bitterly among themselves. The Baganda court was divided almost equally between converts to Catholicism and converts to Protestantism. The Kabaka's life became even more difficult than before, with two opposing factions to contend with, as well as Muslims lurking on the northern frontier. He retaliated by refusing to be converted himself, and by ordering the missionaries not to leave the court at Mmengo.

Both Catholics and Protestants seem to have been more concerned with the interests of their countries than with that of the Church. They were known by the Baganda as the "franza" and the "ingleza," and were thought to preach two different religions.

Mutesa died in 1885, and was succeeded as Kabaka by his son Mwanga. Mwanga too refused to be converted to Christianity and became convinced that the missionaries were plotting to destroy his kingdom. There was a legend among the Baganda that only an invasion from the east could really destroy their state, and Mwanga believed the legend. In October 1885, he heard that the new Anglican bishop, Hannington (1847-1885), was on his way to take over his diocese, and was approaching Uganda from what are now the Kenya Highlands in the east. Mwanga promptly had the bishop murdered, as a legendary "conquering devil," and then tried to massacre all the Christians, native and European, at his court.

Mwanga's rebellion united the two Christian factions again, and the Kabaka was held prisoner while his Muslim followers were fought in a bitter war on the shores of Lake Victoria. In 1890 Lugard arrived at the head of an expedition of the Imperial British East Africa Company, which had been granted the right to rule the area in the name of the British government. Lugard brought the war to a successful end, as he had with his first campaign in Nyasaland, and declared Uganda a protectorate of the Company.

The declaration of the protectorate did not please either Mwanga or the Catholic French missionaries and traders. In 1892 Lugard, with the only machine gun in East Africa, had to fight a savage war against the French to establish British Protestant supremacy. The bills for the war were paid by the Church Missionary Society in London. In an attempt to prevent any further disgraceful wars between Christian denominations, the court was reorganized to give Catholics and Protestants equal shares in the government. There were two First Ministers, two Generals and so on, a comical situation but one which did guarantee an uneasy peace among the Baganda. The other peoples of Uganda did more or less as they pleased until Sir Harry Johnston arrived in 1899 to "put things in order."

As in Nyasaland, Johnston believed that peace could only be made permanent, and a multiracial society created, if Europeans settled and became "white

Ugandans." He was optimistic about the possibility of realizing this ideal. The religious squabbles between the "franza" and the "ingleza" seemed to have become less bitter after the shameful war of 1892. Sixty per cent of the Baganda were Christian, and they had their own ordained priests by 1896, who lived and worked on equal terms with European priests. Slavery had been abolished and both Catholic and Protestant schools had been started.

The important thing was to organize the government properly, collect taxes for building roads and schools, and establish Protestant farmers on land that was ideal for raising coffee, cotton, sugar and tea. In his letters to London, Johnston listed these advantages, and pointed out that the climate was agreeable (60-80°F. all the year round with 50 inches of rain a year), with excellent potential for a prosperous country. He suggested that the mountains to the west of the Ugandan plateau might well be rich in minerals such as copper, wolfram and beryl.

In 1900, the government in London approved Johnston's proposals for "settlement and resettlement." He gave one square mile of land to each of the principal chiefs (Bakungu) and many of the lesser chiefs, in return for a tax payment every year for every hut and gun on the land. He accepted responsibility for drainage of swamps and the conservation of forests, and committed the Protectorate administration to work closely with a parliament (Lukiiko) composed of these chiefs or their representatives.

Johnston did not realize that he was destroying the old feudal system by making the chiefs the owners of their land instead of tenants of the Kabaka. Kabakas had always kept the Baganda aristocracy under control by holding over them the threat that the land which gave them their political power might be taken away. In this way Kabakas had been able to protect the poor, landless peasants and tenants of the Bakungu and lesser chiefs (Batangole). Johnston made it necessary for the Bugandan and Federal Ugandan governments to increase their political activity in order to protect the poor and keep the new landed aristocracy loyal to the Ugandan Federation.

Nevertheless, the new arrangement gave the country a stable and efficient government, even if it did number the days of the now powerless Kabakas. Buganda, the most important state in Uganda, made spectacular progress in school and hospital building, without any assistance from the British government. By the beginning of the First World War, the country had the largest number of technical and teacher-training colleges in Africa, and probably the largest number of literate Africans. By 1914, much of the civil service was African, and European control of the government was more formal than real. The British government's main contribution to the development of the Protectorate was the construction of a railway from the coast to the interior. The railway made it possible to import machinery, as well as a variety of foods to supplement the native diet. It also put an end to slavery once and for all when it became cheaper to send goods by rail than to use slave porters.

The building of the Uganda railway, 1895-1900, had an unforeseen consequence. East of Uganda was an unknown and hostile territory which had been proclaimed the British East African Protectorate in 1895. The cost of building some stretches of the railway had been enormously increased due to raids by hostile tribes, especially the Masai. Masai warriors, who were nomadic ranchers, stole the rails which they used in the construction of their fortified cattle pens. They stole the telegraph wires, too, and made them into bracelets and necklaces for their womenfolk.

The Kikuyu, however, who were settled farmers in the Kenya Highlands, were reasonably friendly. Their friendliness did not do them much good. As British farmers explored the Highlands, which seemed more fertile and agreeable than the Ugandan lands Johnston offered them, the Kikuyu found themselves attacked by disease brought in by the British and their Indian servants. In the decade from 1895 to 1905, nearly half the tribe died of smallpox, having been weakened by near starvation following the death of their cattle from rinderpest and the destruction of their crops by locusts. On to the empty Kikuyu farms moved the British who had unwittingly helped to empty them, and thus the colony of Kenya was founded.

Kenya Colony quickly became a paradise for British settlers. The government of the Colony encouraged the immigration of British farmers with substantial amounts of capital, and granted land on 999-year leases. Rich coffee and tea plantations were established, and the railway made it possible for the crops to be moved to port quickly and cheaply. It was also possible to import from England, at a reasonable price, all the home comforts which made life on the temperate plateau quite as agreeable as life in England.

These settlers were not too enthusiastic about the building of schools for the natives, nor about organizing self-government for the Masai, the Kikuyu and other tribes. There was a general feeling that if he were educated and taught to govern himself, the native would "get above himself." But the missions did set up schools and training colleges, especially in and around the capital, Nairobi, and found the Kikuyu apt pupils. But they did not become Christians. About seventy per cent of the population remained pagan throughout the country's colonial history. Education, however, did help to unite a new "de-tribalized" class of native Kenyans. Missionary activity saved the Kikuyu from disintegration as a tribe after the disasters of the last decade of the nineteenth century, and from among them came the future leaders of the "de-tribalized" and "re-tribalized" Africans of the Colony.

The "partition of Africa" at the end of the nineteenth century gave to Germany the territory between Kenya-Uganda and Nyasaland. A vast tract of land—some 360,000 square miles inhabited by more than 120 tribes —it was from the start difficult to administer. The coastal plain, bought from the Sultan of Zanzibar for £200,000*, was relatively easy to settle, but there was only a network of tracks leading to the interior, a plateau dominated by Africa's highest mountain, Kilimanjaro. The one navigable river, the Rufiji, was unexplored. Lakes Victoria and Tanganyika were certainly navigable, but there was always "trouble with the British."

At first the German Kaiser hoped to administer his new colony, known as German East Africa, by handing it over to a charter company, as the British had done in India and elsewhere in Africa. But the only applicants for a charter went bankrupt in a year, and until 1918, the colony was ruled directly from Berlin. Karl Peters (1856-1918), the explorer, was appointed the colony's first

*$1,000,000 at the time.

governor, and seventy army officers were sent out to help him set up the administration. Peters was a good explorer, but a poor administrator. Berlin allotted him little in the way of finance or facilities, and he decided that it was safe to leave his seven million subjects in the hands of the Arabs who were running the slave trade and other, more legitimate, business. This made life very complicated because the government in Berlin insisted that he abolish the slave trade immediately. When he failed to do this, because he depended on the Arabs to collect taxes and organize road construction, complaints from Johnston in Uganda soon reached Berlin.

Peters wanted to settle many German farmers on land around Kilimanjaro, and appropriated two million acres for this purpose. He did not consult the Bantu farmers already living there, but simply dispossessed them. He then resettled them on land elsewhere. A wiser, more tactful man might have made this move more comfortable for the Bantu, but Peters left it to his Arab officials to organize the resettlement. Many Arabs appropriated resettlement land for themselves, turning the Bantu loose as starving, landless laborers.

It was not surprising that, in 1906, there was an open rebellion by the dispossessed Bantu, and in 1907 an inquiry began in Berlin which ended in Peters' deposition. From 1907 until the territory passed to Britain as a Protectorate in 1919 (when its name was changed to Tanganyika Territory), it was administered by Germany justly and sometimes efficiently. There was still a shortage of capital for road and rail building—the railways to the coast had to be rebuilt after five years, because "economies" had made them unusable—but the Bantu were settled as a class of peasant proprietors, each head of a family with six acres of freehold land. The institutes for research in agriculture and tropical medicine established in the territory were undoubtedly the best in Africa. The Arabs lost their privileged position. Local government was returned to the Bantu, assisted by specially trained German district officers. During the period of the British Protectorate, 1919-1946, much of the reformed German administration was to continue more or less unchanged. Agriculture—cotton, coffee, tea, tobacco and sisal—flourished, and the country's mineral resources were explored.

But though Johnston, Lugard, and Peters were giants in the opening-up of East and Central Africa, none of them compares with the bizarre figure of King Leopold of Belgium, who had as his private property an entire African state.

The story of the Congo really begins with Stanley's explorations in 1877. The Portuguese claimed the area as their own, as they did all of Central Africa, but Stanley found no trace of effective occupation. The Portuguese presence in the area was limited to what is now Angola, and to Mozambique on the east coast, and even there, with the abolition of slavery, there was little activity. Stanley's only rivals in the making of treaties with the tribes were the French to the north in present-day Gabon and in Brazzaville in the Congo.

Toward the end of 1877, Stanley and King Leopold, his patron, formed a Committee for the Study of the Upper Congo (later renamed the International Congo Association). The Committee sent out circular letters to philanthropists all over the world, calling for map-making and exploration "in the interests of the natives . . . a crusade worthy of the century of progress." By the time the Berlin Conference met in 1884 to divide Africa among

73

the imperial powers, the Association had published scores of tracts and organized many lectures based on Stanley's work in the field. Britain and Germany were impressed, and in 1885 King Leopold's Committee was recognized as the government of a "Congo Free State." The French, however, were a little uncertain about the manner in which Leopold intended to rule. They themselves had brazenly divided the French Congo into monopoly concessions covering coffee, palm oil and timber. With the aid of these monopolies, the French government hoped to develop the country's resources without paying for anything out of government funds.

King Leopold soon confirmed French suspicions. Under Stanley as Governor-General, the Congo became the king's private property, by the simple device of buying out all other interests, philanthropic or otherwise. It cost the king nearly all his personal fortune to do this, but he was well satisfied. He granted concessions to companies to exploit the country's natural resources, keeping fifty per cent of the shares in each company for himself. He gave land to companies willing to build railways, again keeping fifty per cent of the shares. The railways filled in the gaps in the River Congo's transportation system, linking navigable stretches of the river and bypassing rapids. The more the Congo Free State was opened up to the sea, the more money the king made. In 1900 he put Katanga, a fifth of the Congo, into the hands of a company which not only made the king a fortune but also ruled in his name without any responsibility to the Belgian parliament. In twenty-five years, King Leopold is said to have made a profit of four hundred per cent on his original investment.

In 1908, however, this private kingdom of Leopold's

came under harsh criticism, and the Belgian government insisted on bringing it into the empire as a colony. The government gave the king a vast sum "in gratitude" at the time of the takeover, in spite of the fact that public and private investigations showed that he had ruthlessly exploited the people and resources of the Free State. One writer accused the king of having revived the slave trade, with a system of forced labor ostensibly designed to civilize the natives by teaching them to work. He certainly taxed the natives heavily—each village had to pay sheep, chicken, maize and vegetables to the king's representatives, who had displaced the tribal chiefs and heads of families. The king's favorite, a ruler of the Upper Congo, was a notorious slave trader, Tippoo Tib, who not only taxed but enslaved the Congolese. Until 1908, not one school was opened for the Congolese, and the only medical care available to them was from mission doctors.

Like Peters, Johnston and Lugard, King Leopold saw nothing extraordinary in the fact that one man should rule and exploit territories as large as most of western Europe. Central and East Africa seemed to them "a big place, which called for big men." These men colonized in the firm and sincere belief that it was their duty to do so in the interests of civilization. If several hundred thousand Africans died in the process, and if they themselves became enormously rich, this was the way history naturally unfolded. It was in keeping with the mood of Victorian times that they should think that "all is for the best, in the best of all possible worlds."

6

British settlers in the Cape and Natal; conflict between British and Boers; first Boer War 1880; Cecil Rhodes and Kruger; British South Africa Company; foundation of Rhodesia; the Jameson raid; second Boer War 1899; South Africa entirely within the British Empire; growth and development of Rhodesia; German missionaries in South West Africa; political development of South Africa; South Africa leaves the British Commonwealth 1961

THE BOERS IN SOUTH AFRICA VIEWED WITH ALARM THE activity by Britain, Belgium, France and Germany to the north. They did not feel bound by the decisions of the 1884 Conference, which assumed it had the right to partition Africa. After all, Boer exploration, trek, and settlement had opened up the first large tracts of Africa to Europeans. Yet there was no Boer representative at the Conference in Berlin. In the Boers' South African Republic (Transvaal), it was thought to be only a plot to give the British greater strength in their struggle to dominate all of Africa south of the Zambezi. The only "bright light" was the German annexation of South West Africa in the year of the Conference. The Germans were at least sympathetic.

Certainly, the leaders of the British communities in Natal and the Cape had not inspired confidence, at least in their honesty and tolerance.

The men who had settled in Natal had been brought out from England by a man named Byrne, a dishonest Liverpool-Irish cattle dealer. These English settlers, who had driven the Boers across the Vaal, knew nothing about local conditions, and in some cases nothing about farming. They grew the wrong crops, and their ·good sugar was too expensive without the use of native labor; yet this native labor was forbidden by the Anglican Bishop Colenso (1814-1883). Eventually, thousands of low-caste Indians were imported, creating further racial conflict.

In the Cape, a succession of British High Commissioners had broken most of the agreements made with the Boers at the 1854 Blomfontein Convention. Though Britain was supposed to have no claims to land beyond the Orange River, the High Commission claimed Griqualand as soon as the first diamond was found there in 1867. The president of the South African Republic, M. W. Pretorius, and the leader of the Griquas, Nicholas Waterboer, protested, but an Arbitration Commission awarded direct control of the new diamond mines to the government in London. Pretorius, who had trusted the Arbitration Commissioner, was removed from office.

Furthermore, the Cape government, supported by London, controlled the road north from the Cape to the Boer republics, and refused to allow the building of another outlet to the sea at Mozambique. This further impoverished the Transvaal. Only the Orange Free State, led by its President, J. H. Brand (1823-1888), achieved some prosperity supplying food to the diamond diggers in their "capital," Kimberley. In 1880, when the diamond fields were placed under administration from the Cape (now a self-governing colony), the British threat seemed even more menacing. Perhaps even the market for food would soon be lost to the Boers.

A few Boers and British settlers realized that this constant conflict could not continue. Lord Carnarvon, (1831-1890), gave the Orange Free State £90,000 compensation for the loss of the expropriated Griqua diamond fields; during his time as Colonial Secretary (1874-1878), he encouraged co-operation between the Cape Dutch, led by Jan Hofmeyr (1845-1909), and settlers like Cecil Rhodes (1853-1902), who were gaining control of the diamond fields and the Cape parliament. Indeed, the British and Boers even fought a war together against the Zulus in 1879.

Boer purists, however, did not welcome any Anglo-Boer co-operation. They resented any attempt by the Cape Dutch to move closer to the British, and resented in particular a proposal to change the language of the Church to the Taal dialect (a mixture of Dutch and English, with a simplified grammar).

At the end of 1880 the Boers took up arms and the first Boer War began. The number of British troops in the Transvaal was very small and they were no match for the Boers who knew their country well. The majority of the British force was defeated at Majuba Hill and Laing's Nek, and as both sides were anxious to end the war by then, the British government called a conference at Pretoria. In a Convention signed in 1881 the independence of the Transvaal as the South African Republic, under the suzerainty of the Queen, was recognized. This was ratified at the London Convention of 1884 after certain terms had been modified. Although all mention of the Queen had been omitted, the Convention also restricted the powers of the Transvaal, which provoked discontent and protest. However, Paul Kruger (1825-1904), the president of the Transvaal, was determined to abolish all such restrictions.

Between 1884 and 1895, British South Africa and the Transvaal co-existed uneasily.

Paul Kruger, 1825-1904. First President of the South African
Republic 1882-1901 *Photo: courtesy South African Embassy*

Cecil Rhodes (1853-1902)
Photo: Radio Times Hulton Picture Library

Cecil Rhodes, then Prime Minister of the Cape, was the moving spirit behind British expansion. He worked hard at making a fortune for himself, as well as on the project of creating a "little British Empire" from the Zambezi to the Cape. He made treaties with the chiefs in Zululand and Bechuanaland, immediately following the Berlin Conference, and consolidated Britain's hold on the ports and the road north from the Cape, effectively isolating the Transvaal. His intention seems to have been to starve the Boers into submission. He boasted that in the year following the Berlin Conference his own personal income was greater than that of the Transvaal, and it was no idle boast. His company, De Boers, which he alone controlled after he had bought out his partner and greatest rival, provided the world's diamonds.

But President Kruger was not an easy man to subdue or starve into submission. He founded new Boer republics in alliance with his own, and was soon the acknowledged leader of all the Boers in South Africa. In 1886 his resistance was stiffened by the discovery of gold on the Witwatersrand. The city of Johannesburg, granted a charter in September of that year, soon grew to be the most important city on the continent. Diamond diggers and prospectors who were uncomfortable under Rhodes' monopoly rule left Kimberley and settled in the new city, even though the Boers refused to grant them any civil rights and taxed them heavily. Kruger passed laws in the Volksraad giving the monopoly of all miners' supplies to the government, quickly increasing the revenues by a thousand per cent. Worse, as far as Rhodes was concerned, Kruger sent diplomats into Matabeleland (a Zulu settlement) to the north and made treaties with Chief Lobengula (1836-1894), acquiring rights to dig for gold at Tati, and freedom from interference for Boer goods traveling north.

Rhodes was alarmed by the success of Kruger's various enterprises. He had his eye on Matabeleland (now part of Rhodesia) as an extension of Cape Colony, and was furious to think that the Matabele had concluded a treaty with the anti-native Boers. He sent one of his friends to negotiate a new treaty with Lobengula in 1888, which made the territory a British Protectorate.

Through his friends in Holland, Kruger tried to convince the British government that Rhodes was a man with an insatiable appetite for power, who could not be trusted to work in the interests of the natives. But this attempt to curb Rhodes failed. In October 1889, the British South Africa Company was granted a charter, with Rhodes as chairman, and given both political and economic authority over all of present-day Zambia and Rhodesia. In 1890, an expedition led by Rhodes' friend Dr. L. S. Jameson (1853-1917), arrived in Matabeleland, founded the city of Salisbury, and proclaimed the "Rhodes Charterland" or Rhodesia. At the same time, one of the Company's agents reached the Congolese frontier and claimed a part of Katanga, laying the foundations of the copper mining industry in the future Northern Rhodesia. By the spring of 1891, Rhodes controlled the British South Africa Company's territory (Rhodes Charterland) and all of Bechuanaland and the Cape, thanks to his enormous economic and political power in the Cape itself. He even had a foothold in Nyasaland.

Kruger did not take the invasion of the British South Africa Company without protest. He began to build his own railway through Swaziland to the Portuguese port of Lourenço Marques, and helped finance another from the

Cape to Johannesburg. He also began new negotiations with Lobengula, hoping to prove to an international court that Rhodes had claimed land already within the sphere of influence of an established state, the South African Republic. The Lourenco Marques Railway was opened in 1894, and the Republic achieved independence of the Cape and Natal ports. Kruger also effectively stopped all attempts by Rhodes to buy control of mining operations on the Rand—the government monopolies of miners' supplies made it a waste of money to make commercial attacks on the Republican government.

In 1894, Rhodes began to look for ways to force Kruger to submit to the British Crown, so it would be possible to create a single colony from the frontiers of Rhodes Charterland to the Cape. In 1894, Jameson defeated Lobengula in battle and removed the one hope Kruger had of claiming the Matabele zone of the Charterland. Later that year, Rhodes founded the National Union Movement, which was intended as a rallying point for non-Boers living in the South African Republic without civil rights of any kind. Rhodes hoped for a rebellion by these disenfranchised miners, who filled the Republic's treasury without being able to vote, so that he could annex the Republic "in defense of democratic rights." But Rhodes was unlucky. The British government in London was averse to these machinations, and the non-Boers, or Uitlanders, were not enthusiastic about the possibility of losing the source of their income. Kruger increased the pressure on the Uitlanders, and strengthened his own hold on the lines of communication with the Cape by closing the fords over which Cape traffic passed to avoid the expensive railway to the south.

In December 1895, Rhodes decided to gamble on the

Young Zulu warrior in traditional dress
Photo: courtesy South African Embassy

loyalty to the National Union Movement of at least some of the Uitlanders. He sent Jameson with a troop of British South Africa Company police to march on Johannesburg. By the time he had realized the rashness of the order, it was too late to recall Jameson, who was a day's march into the Transvaal on December 29th. Kruger reacted quickly, notwithstanding a report that the British government was already sending some troops to support any Uitlander rebellion. Jameson was captured on January 2, 1896, by the Boer general Cronje (1835-1911), and handed over in triumph to the Cape authorities as a brigand. The Kaiser in Berlin sent a telegram congratulating Kruger, and sent a battleship to lie off the East African coast in support of the Republic. The governments of Russia, France and the United States refused to recognize any British right to take further action to subdue the South African Republic or protect her subject Uitlanders there. The Orange Free State signed an alliance with the Republic, and Cape Dutch leaders left home to serve Kruger on "free Boer land."

Rhodes' failure brought him disgrace. The government in London took over the administration of Rhodes Charterland, dividing it into two regions, each with a Commissioner responsible to the High Commissioner at the Cape. Rhodes still had tremendous economic influence. He built a railway linking Salisbury with the Portuguese port of Beira, making Rhodesia independent of the South African Republic, but his political career was at an end.

Kruger believed that he had won all the battles. He made treaties with many European countries which recognized his country's independence, re-equipped his army and consolidated the alliance with the Orange Free State. Not even an economic slump on the Rand could lessen his popularity, and in 1898 he was re-elected president of the Republic with an enormous majority. He appointed extremist Boers to his government and increased the Uitlanders' taxes, warning them than they could expect no protection from the British government so far away.

Kruger's re-election infuriated the new British High Commissioner in Capetown, Sir Alfred Milner (1852-1925). In February 1899, he informed Kruger that many of his actions were unconstitutional, and that although nominally independent, the South African Republic was still subject to British suzerainty. Nobody was quite sure what this meant, and it had not been defined in the various meetings between Boer and British leaders. It had not been mentioned at all at the last meeting in London in 1884. In June 1899, Milner met Kruger and the Orange Free State's President Steyn, (1857-1916), at Blomfontein. He demanded British control over the Republic's foreign affairs, equal rights for Uitlanders, and the right to review the Republic's internal affairs, including their dealings with natives.

Neither Kruger nor Steyn would accept Milner's demands. The Blomfontein Conference dragged on until September, with Kruger convinced that the British government intended to invade the Republic whatever the outcome. Steyn was anxious to submit the whole dispute to arbitration, but Milner would not agree. Kruger heard that 10,000 additional British troops had already left for South Africa and he had no doubt of their intentions. He told Steyn to drop all ideas of arbitration, sent an ultimatum to Queen Victoria, and mobilized the Boer commandos. On October 12, 1899, war between Britain and the Republic broke out.

The British government certainly underestimated the strength of the Boer forces and their determination to fight. It was not until February, 1900, that Lord Roberts (1832-1914), the Commander-in-chief, succeeded in organizing a steady advance north from the Cape, capturing Kimberley and Blomfontein before he was halted. Regrouping their forces under General Botha (1862-1919) and General De Wet (1854-1922), the Boers held the line until May, when the numerical odds against them became too great. Johannesburg and Pretoria fell in June, and the leader of the governments of the Orange Free State and the South African Republic fled to Holland. By Christmas, Lord Roberts could report that the situation had been stabilized and that the Transvaal and Orange Free State had been annexed as colonies. He returned home to a hero's welcome.

However, the Boers had no intenion of surrendering their independence so easily. Though the British had restored stability to the cities, Boer commandos still roamed the countryside, fighting a guerilla war. Lord Kitchener, (1850-1916), took over command of the British forces. He divided the countryside into zones, and cleared them of Boers one by one. He burned crops and farmhouses, exiled prisoners to St. Helena (and even Ceylon), and put women and children in concentration camps. With this policy of total war, Kitchener succeeded in destroying most Boer resistance by April 1902, and on May 31 the "Peace of Vereeniging" was signed in Pretoria.

But total war, though effective, created its own problems. 250,000 Boers had to be resettled on the land. They had to be helped in the rebuilding of their farms and in the buying of new equipment. New herds of cattle had to be established. The bitterness of the Boers was

87

increased in 1904 when more than 40,000 Chinese laborers were imported, further complicating the problem of race relations. Even worse was the regulation making English again a compulsory language in all schools, though Milner (High Commissioner until 1906) knew that this regulation would only succeed in making the extremist Boers even more hostile. In fact, that is what happened. Het Volk, an extremist party, quickly grew in strength, and notwithstanding their poverty, the Boers set up Dutch-speaking schools of their own for their children.

The whole of South Africa was part of the British Empire, but that fact gave little satisfaction to anybody. The struggle for independence by the Boers continued, and was supported by some British politicians in London and at the Cape who realized that the whole tragic Boer war had been a mistake.

The situation in Rhodesia, which was formerly Rhodes Charterland, was different. The Rhodesians, divided into two regions (Nothern Rhodesia and Southern Rhodesia) were indisputably loyal to the British Crown, and they worked hard to make the colonies prosperous. Capital came from Britain, and from the savings of settlers themselves. The copper mines in Northern Rhodesia were deepened, and proved as rich as those in neighboring Katanga. What was perhaps even more important, agriculture prospered in Southern Rhodesia, attracting more and more new settlers.

While problems of racial conflict were always serious in the newly-pacified South Africa, the Rhodesias seemed to be mercifully free of this disturbing factor. Of course, the population of Rhodesia consisted of only two races, the native and the European. There were not large numbers of Chinese, Indians, Malayans and half-castes, as there were to the south. Thus the British settlers were able to work out a pattern of peaceful co-existence with the natives. White men and native Rhodesians worked together on the plantations (tobacco for the most part). While white Rhodesians were the owners, they soon gave Africans responsible executive posts on the plantations and in the cities of Salisbury and Bulawayo. It was only after work that the racial distinctions became apparent. The boss returned to his bungalow with his native servants and the other Africans went off to their townships. There was no mixing of the races in private houses, but there were multiracial public dining rooms and bars.

The fact that the Boer War had scarcely touched the Rhodesias also contributed to prosperity and stability. There had been no destruction of farms and plantations, so agriculture was able to take up its natural rhythm and profit from the ruin of the Boer farms. Exports of food to the Transvaal increased during the years of the resettlement of the Boers, and there were no political complications inside Rhodesia to interfere with trade. In addition, there were no "poor whites" to plague them. The "poor whites" in South Africa—impoverished by the war or by misfortune—were a drain on all of the white community. They also worsened relations between whites and natives in general, because an unwritten social law said that all whites must be paid more than natives, whatever their real worth as laborers might be. In Rhodesia this problem did not exist. The whites had all the capital, and all of them were reasonably prosperous, while the natives supplied the labor.

Milner and some liberals in England hoped that the Rhodesias would join with Transvaal, the Orange River Colony (as the Orange Free State was now called), Natal, the Cape and Bechuanaland to form one single colony which could later be transformed into a dominion like Canada or Australia. Other British politicians wanted the Rhodesias to join the other colonies to make sure that there would always be a British, as opposed to a Boer, majority. Great projects for mass immigration from England, however, came to nothing, as all of Great Britain was enjoying prosperity, and the project to join the British Rhodesias with South Africa came to nothing, too. There were too many differences of religion, of economic status and political belief to make the proposition attractive to Rhodesians, even African Rhodesians. It is interesting to note that native Africans—and not only the Mashona and Matabele who were traditionally Rhodesian—elected to go to Rhodesia from neighboring Belgian, British and Boer colonies.

After the Boer War, German interest in South West Africa declined. This was perhaps not surprising. The colony was mostly desert—318,000 square miles with scarcely one person per square mile. Virtually no agriculture was possible. Cattle raising was the only source of food and trade, and the eastern region, a part of the Kalahari Desert, formed an impassable barrier to the importation of food products. The natives kept themselves alive on grubs and fish from the sea and rivers. There was a feeling that there were large deposits of diamonds, manganese, zinc and lead, but capital from Germany was not readily forth-coming to make the proper geological surveys or to open up pilot mines.

What was surprising was the intensity of the missionary effort in this inhospitable place. Notwithstanding the heat and lack of rain, thousands of German Lutheran pastors visited the colony, and before the First World

War had converted nearly half the population. There was less effort by the Catholics, but it was still notable for South Africa. The Boer Republics and British colonies had always been infertile soil for Roman Catholic missionary work, but German South West Africa soon boasted a Catholic population of ten per cent.

Of all the regions of Africa, the south, though completely colonized, was in the state of the greatest uncertainty in the early years of the twentieth century. Though there were optimists in London who believed, in 1910, that the new Union of South Africa could absorb Boer discontent, there were also many pessimists. The pessimists were to be proved right.

In 1912, J. B. M. Hertzog (1866-1942), founded a Nationalist Party. He declared that the only future for South Africa was as a Boer Republic, and he recommended that schoolchildren be taught both English and Afrikaans in preparation for that day. In 1924, Hertzog came to power at the head of a Nationalist-Labour party coalition. It is important to remember that in South Africa the poor-white Labour Party supporters were unashamed racists and wanted Negroes barred from all "white" jobs. It is also important to remember that the South African Communist Party, on Moscow's orders, also opposed integration of white and black.

The only opposition to Hertzog's nationalism came from Jan Smuts (1870-1950), who led the South African Party, later the United Party. Smuts differed in his views from Hertzog only in so far as the United Party was pro-British. He opposed Hertzog's "cultural program"—the recognition of Afrikaans as an official language—but for the rest he believed, too, in the separation of the races. There was so little fundamental difference between

91

Jan Christian Smuts, 1870-1950
Photo: courtesy South African Embassy.

Hertzog and Smuts that in 1932 the two men joined forces to lead the so-called United South African National Party in a coalition government. The coalition survived, to repair the economic damage done by the slump of 1930, until 1939.

In 1939, the extent of anti-British and pro-German feeling among Afrikaaners was revealed. There had been for several years pro-Nazi Gray Shirts, Black Shirts and storm troopers, but it was a shock to many when the South African Parliament voted to join Britain in the war against Germany by only eighty votes to sixty-seven. Hertzog, with his friends Daniel F. Malan (1874-1959) and Pirow, left the government, which was carried on by Smuts and his pro-British friends alone.

After the Second World War, South Africa went to the polls in 1948 to choose its "peace government." Smuts, the war leader, hoped to be returned, especially as the Nationalist opposition was campaigning on a platform of "apartheid," the "choice between white rule with racial purity, and total immersion in a black sea." The war leader was rejected, and the Nationalists won. Malan became prime minister, followed by Johannes G. Strijdom (1893-1958), in 1954, and Hendrik Verwoerd (1901-1966), in 1957. At the 1958 elections, the Nationalists won 103 out of 156 seats in Parliament. The policy of apartheid was slowly but inexorably implemented. Special laws were passed for "non-whites," special passes became compulsory, and "separate education and cultural development" was established. Any active opposition to apartheid was dubbed "Communistic," and members of the opposition tried for treason.

It was inevitable that South Africa should be forced out of the multiracial British Commonwealth, and this happened in 1961. A referendum was held in that year, which confirmed that a majority of South African whites favored republican status for their country. The Commonwealth Conference, asked to approve the proclamation of the Republic on May 31, 1961, tried to associate approval with a request for an end to "oppression of the natives." At this, Verwoerd walked out of the Conference, and South Africa thereafter ceased to be a member of the Commonwealth.

In spite of world opposition, the Republic of South Africa continues to thrive, due largely to its resources of gold and precious stones and the efficient management of its economy. The Republic even enjoys good relations with some Black African states, notably the former High Commission Territories of Basutoland and Bechuanaland, which became independent in 1966 as Lesotho and Botswana. There seems to be little popular enthusiasm in Europe for a "war of liberation of the African Negro," however fiercely some politicians denounce the Republic. It may well be that the world is tired of "wars of liberation" and every other sort of war.

7

Europeans in West Africa; extension of French influence; Gold Coast under British rule; war with the Ashanti; British and French trading . companies in West Africa; Taubman Goldie; economic competition between Britain and France; exploitation of Nigeria; establishment of Nigerian Federation; German, Spanish and Portuguese interests in the area

WEST AFRICA HAD BEEN FOR CENTURIES THE SUPPLY center for the slave trade serving European plantations in America. Little attempt had been made to settle Europeans on the West African coast, which was known as the white man's grave. Traders carried on dealings of a sort with the tribes, in gold and palm oil, but when the slave trade was abolished both traders and governments lost interest in the coast. There was interest on the part of the missionaries, however, who were determined to see for themselves that the slave trade had been abolished. These missionaries were in the main British, German and French—the Swedes, Danes, Portuguese and Dutch quietly dropped the whole area as soon as their nationals were forbidden to buy and ship slaves.

French Catholic missionaries believed that it was possible to convert all the tribes in West Africa, starting from the base in Senegal. Europeans were successfully growing cotton in Senegal, and got on well with the natives. It was felt that a sustained effort could link up French West Africa with the territories under French influence on the North African coast, to create one "Gallic

Christian culture bloc." Unfortunately for the missionaries, Muslim zealots were anxious to remove the last traces of European occupation and establish a "Muslim Arab-Negro culture bloc," extending from the Nile to the Gulf of Guinea. The Toucouleur and Bambara tribes were the spearhead of the drive to purge West Africa of the infidel. These tribes were led by descendants of the Ahmadu who had led the "holy war" in the early years of the nineteenth century, and by Samory, a born general of the Mandingo who had made a name for himself though he had no chief's blood in his ancestry.

In 1854, Napoleon III agreed to organize a large-scale military expedition against the Toucouleur and Bambara, and sent General Louis Faidherbe (1818-1899) to lead the expedition. With the support of Wolof tribesmen, many of them already converted to Christianity, General Faidherbe slowly pushed back the frontier of Islam, proclaiming French sovereignty over vast areas of West Africa as far as Lake Chad. By 1874, French troops were far away from the original cotton and palm oil plantations they had set out to defend, and thousands of Catholic missionaries were building churches, often converting mosques, on the grasslands on the southern borders of the Sahara.

British Protestant missionaries, and the few traders, were alarmed at the rate of French expansion. The British government did not see that it was any of its business. All over Africa it was being forced to declare protectorates, adding to the expense of running the British Empire which was expanding at an even more alarming rate than the French. Most British politicians were anti-empire, some for humane reasons, others because they were afraid that a large empire would bring about a higher income tax. Nevertheless, there were two colonies on the West African coast—Sierra Leone and the Gold Coast—and it was obviously not right that the French should surround them like a hostile jungle. There was also some alarm at the way in which Germans were consolidating their position to the east of the Gold Coast, in what was to become German Togoland.

At first, a succession of British governments told the Gold Coast merchants that they could consider themselves protected only along the coast itself. This limitation was confirmed, even when in 1873 the Ashanti tribes to the north of the colony attacked British forts garrisoned by British and Fanti troops. The colony's semi-private army, subsidized by the government in London, defeated the Ashanti and wanted to occupy the interior. They felt that it would be useful to dominate a complete slice of Africa extending from the coast to the River Niger, effectively stopping any French advance to the east. The British government refused to permit this, and ordered instead that the Ashanti should pay an indemnity and promise good behavior. However, in 1895, a more imperialistic government in London decided to proclaim a protectorate over the interior north of the Ashanti, partly to stop any further French or German advance and partly because British merchants were trading there.

At this point the governor of the Gold Coast, Sir Frederic Hodgson (1851-1925), ordered the Ashanti paramount chief, Prempeh, to guarantee freedom of transit across the territory for all British merchants bound for the Northern Protectorate. One of the govenor's clerks also discovered that the 1874 indemnity had not been paid, and a missionary at Accra told lurid tales of cannibalism and human sacrifices in the Ashanti. The governor obligingly added demands that these practices must cease, and that the indemnity should be paid immediately, to his demand for freedom of transit.

Prempeh was thus in a difficult position. He was the "asantehene," or paramount chief of the Ashanti, but he was not chief of all the Ashanti tribes. Ashanti was rather like the United States, a federation, and the individual states had even more power than their American counterparts. Prempeh could not order the other chiefs, the heads of the states, to contribute to any indemnity; in any event, the federal treasury was usually empty. Moreover, he had no control over practices such as human sacrifice among the member states of the Ashanti. But most important, the lesser chiefs were putting pressure on him to stop German, British and French merchants from tramping back and forth across what was supposed to be an independent country.

In 1896, in response to this last pressure, Prempeh closed the frontiers of the Ashanti to all foreigners. The Gold Coast governor ordered that they be reopened, and when they were not, he sent an army to sack the Ashanti federal capital, Kumasi. The temples were looted, and the 1874 indemnity thus "collected." Prempeh was deported.

Sir Frederic Hodgson now expected peace to the north of the colony, but in order to convince the natives in their own terms, he decided to mount a search for the Golden Stool. He was certain that this was a throne of some kind, and that once Queen Victoria had sat on it, the Ashanti would recognize her as their Protectress and there would be no more trouble. However, the Golden Stool of the Ashanti was actually a holy symbol which embodied all the spirits of the dead, and an asantehene would sooner have died than commit the sacrilege of sitting on it. The idea of enthroning a white queen on the Golden Stool horrified the Ashanti tribes to such an extent that they not only hid it, but rebelled in 1901 against their new Protectress. Defeated in 1902, the Ashanti became colonial subjects of the Crown and, as their historians say, "were never free again."

Farther along the West African coast, the nineteenth century also ended in a wave of war and annexation.

The French had pressed on around the Northern Protectorate of the Gold Coast, founding settlements and claiming colonies in the Upper Volta and along the Lower Niger. They had also marched north from the French Congo, settling Gabon. Germans had occupied the territory north of Gabon, the Cameroons, as well as Togoland bordering the Gold Coast Colony.

British merchants in the city of Lagos—a British colony since 1861—were worried about the prospect of competition sponsored by other governments, and pleaded with the government in London to "pacify" the whole area of the Lower Niger. As in the case of the Gold Coast, successive governments in London showed great reluctance to take on new colonial commitments. There was a consul on the island of Fernando Po, and he would have to do. Any despatch of troops of civil servants might raise the rate of the income tax at home, and this would prove very unpopular.

Luckily for the British merchants, one of them, Taubman Goldie (1846-1925), had empire-building dreams as vivid as those of Cecil Rhodes in South and Central Africa. Goldie's dreams, however, were not always decorated with his country's flag. He believed that the important thing was to make sure that British merchants

99

had the monopoly of all profitable trade in the Niger Delta and adjoining areas. It did not matter which government looked after the policing, or colored the map green, red or yellow. Africans did not understand the subtle difference between a Union Jack and a French tricolor. If anything, they took advantage of the political quarrels between Europeans. For the merchants, Africans were easier to deal with if they were sure where the money was. They measured power "like gold, by the ounce," as Goldie did. This at any rate was Goldie's firm belief, and he acted on it.

Both Goldie and Rhodes understood better than most of their contemporaries the management of joint stock companies. They knew that ownership of capital is not the same thing as control of capital. Throughout Africa,

Sir George Taubman Goldie (1846-1925)
Photo: Radio Times Hulton Picture Library

a great deal of money had been invested in trading companies which were managed by men who themselves possessed little. Goldie, starting with the small firm of Holland, Jacques and Company, spun a web of companies which gave him control over nearly all commerce on the Delta. In the process he became a rich man, but his own contribution was that of commercial organizer—talking other companies into stopping "wasteful" competition, setting up central offices to do the work of accountancy for several companies, centralizing offices for dealing with the natives. Between 1877 and 1882 he created the largest commercial empire in West Africa, the National Africa Company.

French capitalists, who had the ear of their government, were not afraid of British government interference in West Africa. Most of West Africa was already French and any activity in the Gold Coast Colony on the part of the London government seemed to them pathetic. But they were afraid of Goldie, who had incorporated into his National Africa Company many French commercial corporations, and who seemed likely to swallow up many more. In 1882 they persuaded the president of France, Léon Gambetta (1838-1882), to invest his own immense fortune in the French Equatorial Africa Company, a commercial empire which they hoped would rival Goldie's. For two years the two corporations fought battles of balance sheets, prices, costs and freights. Both corporations had private armies, which protected their trade routes. Neither corporation was averse to burning the other's warehouses or to murdering the other's agents. But the final battles were fought in the counting houses, and in 1884, Goldie emerged the victor, bankrupting the French Equatorial Africa Company.

The British Foreign Office was disturbed when the French government complained about Goldie's trading operations. Liberal civil servants at the Foreign Office thought it was scandalous that one man should wield such power without being responsible to anyone. Missionaries in Lagos warned that he was a godless man who was corrupting the youth of the colony.

In April 1884, a new consul was appointed to control all of the Niger Delta. Hewett, a man of high moral standing, would be stationed at Calabar, the principal missionary center for the Niger Delta. He was told that a conference would be held shortly, at which time Africa would be divided among the principally interested European powers, and his special task was to annex as much of the area as possible. He was also told that there were even kings of the Cameroons anxious to be placed under British protection. Nobody told Goldie that a man was being sent out to overrule him.

When Goldie heard that Hewett was on his way, he was furious. Goldie wanted the political chaos along the coast to continue; it meant larger profits for him, for the tribesmen were never sure to which white man they should complain. Goldie got in touch with a German firm, the Wormann Gesellschaft, in which he had an interest; he told them that it would be a good idea for the German government to send out a consul post haste to annex some of the areas to the east and west of the Niger Delta. Togoland already had a strong German presence, and so did the Cameroons. The Wormann Gesellschaft went to work, and persuaded the German government to send out its own "Stanley," a man named Gustav Nachtigal (1834-1885). Though Nachtigal left Europe three weeks after Hewett, he reached the West African coast before his more leisurely rival. He formally annexed Togoland, which had been informally annexed years before; then jumping over the Niger Delta where Hewett was being royally entertained, he landed in the Cameroons five days before Hewett realized that he had any competition in the business of flag-raising on the coast. So Britain lost the chance to proclaim a protectorate over the whole of present-day Nigeria and the Cameroons, a loss which earned for her unfortunate consul-extraordinary the nickname of "Too-late Hewett."

Goldie was not financially interested in the Cameroons. He was, however, very much interested in the Nigerian interior, not so much because he believed that there were any resources to exploit there, but because he believed that a friendly Hausa-Niger interior would give his agents peace in the Delta. He offered the British government a guarantee that he would bring the interior under control, at no expense to the British taxpayer; in return, however, he wanted a charter giving his company (the National Africa Company) the monopoly of all trade and exploitation of resources in "Hausaland" (the Hausa are the major tribe in the north). The British government accepted the offer, and the Royal Niger Company, a subsidiary of the National Africa Company, was chartered in 1886. Goldie was warned to respect the terms of the 1884 Berlin agreements on spheres of influence. German traders were not to be upset; the French were to be politely restrained.

In 1889, the French, still smarting at the way in which Goldie had out-maneuvered and then bankrupted their French Equatorial Africa Company, mustered an armed expedition to force their way into the Niger Delta. Their aim was to find ways of joining their Dahomean protectorate to their territories flanking the Upper Niger, but they were foiled by Goldie, his private army and his Patani tribal allies. The defeat of the French encouraged the Dahomean tribes to revolt, and until the spring of 1894, all French energies were used up in re-establishing law and order over the vast areas of their West African colonies.

Goldie hoped that, having been taught a lesson, the French would stop trying to expand, and would content themselves with the territories confirmed as theirs at the Berlin Conference. He was soon disillusioned. He had reports of a massing of French troops on the Upper Niger, and he feared that they would bring pressure on the northern tribes to revoke their treaties with his company. He told his friends that he was at a considerable disadvantage—he was supposed to make the suppression of the last signs of slavery, and conversion to Christianity, conditions for doing business with these tribes. The French, though they were also supposed to be suppressing slavery and spreading Christianity, had conveniently shelved these principles until such time as they were imperial masters of the area. Goldie realized that he needed a stronger, better led army if he were to fight off the coming invasion of the Hausa-Nigerian interior.

In spite of his unpopularity in London, Goldie succeeded in convincing the government that the French threat was an insult to the British flag, as well as a menace to the prosperity of the Royal Niger Company. The government agreed to subsidize the Company's private army, provided it was brought under proper control. Goldie agreed to ask Lugard, who had pacified Nyasaland and Uganda, to take command of the army, which was to be renamed the West African Frontier Force. Lugard arrived at the end of 1894. By the end of 1895, he and

Goldie felt that they were in a strong enough position to make a show of force among those tribes who might possibly change their loyalty from "a respectful affection" for Queen Victoria to submission to the French president. At the end of 1896, Lugard led a full-scale expedition into the interior, subdued the tribes and, by the terms of the Anglo-French peace treaty of 1898, established British supremacy. The French turned northeast and scrambled for present-day Chad as a consolation for the loss of their Nigerian claims.

The Goldie-Lugard expedition, though successful, was conducted without much regard for the rules of war. Protests from missionaries about Goldie's morals and Lugard's ruthlessness were widely publicized in London. In 1899 the charter of the Royal Niger Company was revoked and all of the north became a protectorate. A similar protectorate was established on the Niger coast, though Lagos continued to exist for a little longer as a separate colony. Goldie was mollified by being given virtual control in Africa over a new corporation, the United Africa Company, though control over the corporation's international activities went to Lever Brothers.

Lugard, now Sir Frederick Lugard, was appointed High Commissioner for the Protectorate of Northern Nigeria. He was a wise administrator, though the task of restoring order and "respectful affection" for the British Crown was not easy. He had to effect the final suppression of slave trading among the Hausa, and to discourage desperate French attempts to nibble away at the frontiers of the protectorate. Perhaps even more difficult was the task of pacifying the Hausa and the Fulani aristocracy and giving them a strong government.

Lugard was faced with strong Fulani emirs, always

ready to rebel and as ready to argue. Some of the emirs complained that the French had told them that *their* way of ruling was the most reasonable, and that the Germans had recommended still another. Who was to say that the British way was the best?

The French ruled in the Upper Niger, as elsewhere in Africa, under the assumption that one day all their Africans would become French, having abandoned "primitive" cultural concepts and adopted those of metropolitan France. Chiefs who were stubbornly primitive were dismissed and replaced with others who ruled over local government areas modeled on the French. A French commandant with a civil and military staff acted as overseer of each territory (French West Africa was divided into twenty territories, divisions which suited the convenience of the map-makers rather than respecting tribal areas). Though tribal rulers became little more than civil servants, the Northern Nigerians liked the French system. The French made great efforts to please them, discouraging Christian missionaries in strongly Muslim areas, and even in whole territories.

The Germans had never expected Africans to become German. They did not want to spread German culture. All they wanted was the establishment of law, order and good public health, so that their merchants could conduct their business peacefully. They established local police forces and spent a great deal of money in research on tropical medicine. African chiefs were left to their own devices, and after 1903 were subject to exactly the same laws and penalties as Europeans. Some Northern Nigerian emirs looked enviously at the nearby Cameroons.

Lugard, too, was not concerned with the spread of British culture, but he was not willing to leave Hausa and

Fulani chiefs to their own devices. He knew they would continue trading in slaves and waging private wars if he looked away, and he could not rely on their loyalty. He looked over the members of the Fulani aristocracy and decided that in the main they were more able than the Hausa minor chiefs. He therefore confirmed the Muslim Fulani emirs in their traditional roles as feudal rulers, but gave each emir a miniature British civil service controlled by a "Resident," employed by the civil service as the official representative of the British Crown and adviser to the local ruler. The Residents and other advisers kept a close watch on the emirs, saw that they did not cheat the tax collectors, discouraged them from making private wars by threatening them with British military intervention, and channeled their trade toward the southern Niger Coast Protectorate and away from the French and German merchants. Over a period of years, Lugard succeeded in convincing even hostile emirs like the Sardauna of Sokoto that his system would work. Government was made easy, and nobody attempted to interfere with local customs. Some missionaries were a little doubtful about this indirect rule, and certainly there were slaves in Northern Nigeria, by local custom, until 1960, but much petty corruption and cruelty did disappear.

The governors of the Lagos Colony and Southern Protectorate were not as efficient as Lugard. Merged in 1906, the colony and the protectorate were responsible for a large number of independent tribes who were not enthusiastic about central government. In desperation, succeeding governors ruled without giving traditional chiefs any voice in government. This meant that the Europeans in Lagos, who were members of a Legislative Council which advised the governor, could exploit the resources of the south without taking the interests of the tribes into consideration. Merchant members of the Legislative Council, friends of Goldie (now sick and semi-retired), managed to get approval of schemes which weakened the economy of the south. One project, to build a north-south railway, was nearly ruined by one of Goldie's friends who obtained permission to build a railway from the north to one of the United Africa Company's private ports, not touching the south which needed the rail link most.

In 1912, Lugard, who had gone to Hong Kong as governor, was asked to return and take office as Governor-General of a united Nigeria. He accepted the offer, and the Nigerian Federation soon became a model of law, order and prosperity. Africans were given membership in the Lagos Legislative Council, and as both British and native rulers feared and respected Lugard, some sort of co-operative democracy came into being throughout the new colony.

While British and French, and to a lesser extent German, activity was carving West Africa into colonies, there was a curious lack of activity on the part of the Spanish and Portuguese who had first touched the coast. This inactivity can only be explained in terms of a general apathy in the Iberian peninsula, an apathy that was a direct consequence of the loss of their vast South and Central American colonies. Spain and Portugal were still numb from this loss, even though it had occurred at the beginning of the nineteenth century. Internal chaos, and a half-hearted attempt to make the home economy viable after so many centuries of living off the wealth of the New World, absorbed most of their little remaining energy and ambition. Portugal still had those parts of South and

Central Africa (Angola and Mozambique) which nobody else wanted, the tiny island of Sao Thome (St. Thomas) off the coast of the Congo, the Cape Verde Islands 273 miles west of Dakar, and an uninteresting slice of the Guinea coast. Spain, after the 1884 Berlin Conference, had 102,700 square miles of the Sahara, a malaria-infested enclave (Ifni) south of the Atlas Mountains, and a tenuous hold (not confirmed until 1912) on part of Morocco.

It was not until World War I that Spanish and Portuguese governments began to take a serious interest in their overseas possessions in Africa. During the decade after the war there were many grandiose schemes for exploration of the hinterland in these territories, and dreams of gold and diamonds (especially in Portuguese Guinea); but by that time it was too late. Capital and markets had been earmarked by other imperial nations. The overseas possessions of Spain and Portugal were given the title "overseas provinces." Yet they were less influenced by the twentieth century than most other colonial regions of Africa, until after the Second World War.

8

THOUGH WEST AFRICA WAS THE LAST REGION OF THE continent to be definitively colonized, it was the birthplace of the movement for independence. Perhaps not surprisingly, the first notions of independence, of "Africa for the Africans," were put into the heads of Africans by missionaries.

The nineteenth-century missionary was, by and large, disappointed with the condition of Africa after the abolition of slavery. Slaves had been freed, but what sort of life awaited their children and grandchildren? The French in West Africa did not encourage missionary work intended to educate and convert the native. This sort of activity might upset the local Muslim chiefs and make government more difficult and more expensive. British merchants like Goldie looked at the African in much the same way as the slaveowners had, as cheap labor with which to exploit the natural resources of the area in the interests of British commerce. The Europeans responsible for government were not famous for Christian charity, and they were unlikely to think of the African as their equal in the sight of God. If he were their equal in the sight of God he would necessarily be entitled to the same wages as a European.

Missionaries tended to have an uneasy conscience even about their own activities. Most realistic priests and missionaries admitted that many converts had sought baptism for the wrong reasons. Some had become Christian as a gesture of thanks after treatment in a mission hospital. Others, seeing that both missionaries and employers were white, had been baptized in the hope that the ceremony would open the way to a good job. Whatever the reason for conversion, many Africans found that their new religion cut them off from the life of their tribe and even of their own families. They could no longer take part in ancestor worship or initiation ceremonies. Their women were supposed to cover themselves and not be "indecently exposed." So it came about that a new class of Africans emerged, speaking the language of the white man, wearing clothes designed by the white man for them, loyal during working hours to white employers but without any tribe to be loyal to when the work was done. It was from this class of de-tribalized Africans, mostly living in the towns and cities, that the leaders of African nationalism were to come.

West African missionaries encouraged the de-tribalized Africans to make a new life for themselves. To those who resented the fact that white men had all the best jobs and all the political power, missionaries replied that Sierra Leone and Liberia were genuine African states in which freed slaves had the power and the best jobs; they said that eventually all Africa would be free, and white men would be honored guests and teachers. Missionaries also pointed out that many of the tribes from which the new class was cut off lived in squalor and barbarity. It was true that the health of this new African class was better, and that their children had schools to go to. It was also true that the feudal rulers of the tribes no longer had any hold over the de-tribalized Africans and so could not make them pay taxes or work without pay for the chief. The brightest of the young men of the new class were given special treatment and plans were discussed, at the beginning of the twentieth century, to send some of them to England to school and then to a university.

Records show that many missionaries genuinely believed that the whole continent would one day regain its independence, just as the slaves in America had regained theirs. Leaders of the Anglican Church were anxious that when this day came, the new governments of an independent Africa should be composed of practicing Christians. Most of the white merchants in West Africa did not set a Christian example in their everyday lives, and would abandon the coast as soon as their privileged position disappeared. And there was the ever-present threat of Islam, which appealed to Africans because it did not ask them to give up customs such as polygamy, and had no white gods.

There were sincere attempts made during the early years of the twentieth century to give Africa its own version of Christianity, one which the de-tribalized African could make attractive to his non-Christianized relatives. These attempts involved the printing of Bibles and tracts in which Christ and his disciples were shown as Africans, with black skins. It also involved pressure on the church authorities to ordain as many African priests as possible, and the training of Africans as doctors and engineers so that they could take over much of the lay work of the missions.

But, perhaps inevitably, African nationalism was born out of resentment and anger—resentment of prevailing white domination and anger at the recollection of the centuries of slave trading to which their ancestors had been subjected. The first murmurings of anger came from a British West Indian, Edward Blyden (1832-1912), son of freed slaves, who found that his freedom did not mean much when he was rejected by an American university on the grounds that his color suggested that he would not be able to complete the courses necessary for a degree. Blyden emigrated to West Africa, "home of my ancestors," and settled in Liberia to write books and pamphlets which were openly anti-white.

Unfortunately for Blyden, the "Father of African Nationalism," Liberia was not the ideal place from which to conduct a campaign for freedom for the African. The original freed slaves lived there in some luxury in American-style "colonial" houses. They were owners of vast plantations who persecuted the natives of the interior, even enslaving some of them. This settler aristocracy was fanatically Protestant, and denied religious liberty to other denominations. The political life was corrupt—a single True Whig Party dominating the government and managing elections in its own interests. The government was both corrupt and inefficient, and the economy was propped up by loans from Britain, France and the United States.

Nevertheless, Blyden's writings found a ready market elsewhere in West Africa, and were given direction at the end of the nineteenth century by John Jackson, a Liberian who had left his country in despair to settle in Nigeria. By the time Blyden died in 1912, Jackson's paper, the Lagos *Weekly Record,* had propagated his views throughout English-speaking West Africa. Blyden's attitude to African nationalism was similar to that of the most enlightened missionaries. He was looking for an "African personality," not a dark imitation of European attitudes on social, economic and political life, nor a nostalgic looking-backwards to the old days of tribalism. Neither Blyden nor Jackson was quite sure how this "African personality" should emerge, or what could be done to encourage its development, but the important thing, they believed, was to get the discussion going. Certainly they succeeded in forming discussion societies as well as getting financial backing for scores of African newspapers with small circulations.

Before the First World War, it was generally believed that Africans would be liberated from the white man by an army of freed American Negro slaves, and this belief persisted until the outbreak of World War II.

In 1905, at a Congress of American Negroes, W. E. B. Dubois (1868-1963), the sociologist, and William Taylor, a journalist, popularized the slogan "The Problem of the Twentieth Century is the Color Problem." Jackson, in the Lagos *Weekly Record,* hailed the Congress as the "dawn of emancipation." Even Lenin made a favorable comment, saying that one day "all those under the yoke of imperialism would be freed, and among the vanguard of the liberators would be Africans and Asians."

Three years later, Dubois organized a Pan-African Congress and drew attention to the danger to the Negro of private business empires like that of Rhodes in South Africa. Dubois's two congresses, at first known as the "Niagara Movement," were rechristened "The National Association for the Advancement of Colored People" (NAACP); the members pledged to continue to hold congresses, and to do everything in their power "until the final day of African freedom." Jackson looked forward to "powerful leadership and splendid example" from the American Negro, "newly awakened to his responsibilities in Africa."

However, the American Negro was more concerned with the struggle for equal rights at home in the United States than with the condition of the African Negro. Although Dubois in his paper, the *Crisis,* urged the importance of American Negro leadership, he was nearly always disappointed. He received his most bitter blow in 1919, when only twelve Negroes volunteered to attend a Pan-African Congress in Paris—and they were refused visas by the State Department of the newly-isolationist United States government. Thereafter, the American Negro was never important in the struggle for African independence. Any claims he might have had to be taken seriously were dissipated by the activities of Marcus Aurelius Garvey (1887?-1940).

Garvey was born in Jamaica. He was largely self-educated and read widely if not always wisely. His favorite books were the Old Testament and a life of Napoleon, books which convinced him that he was a Negro cross between Moses and Napoleon, sent to lead the chosen black people out of the wilderness of white captivity to freedom and prosperity in Africa. He was not taken seriously in the West Indies, so he moved to New York in 1916, where he was taken up by some rich Communist Negroes who wanted to embarrass the imperialist powers in Africa. Garvey was urged to proclaim himself president of the first Provisional Government of Africa. He did so, sending messages to prominent Negroes in English-speaking Africa, ordering them to rise against their masters. He awarded titles to his backers and friends in New York—Baron Zambezi, Lord Kenya, Baron Mali were some of them—and decorated "progressives" with the Order of Mozambique. He founded the Universal Negro Improvement and African Communities League, which was to buy land for new settlements in Africa, and incorporated the Black Star Steamship Line, the Universal Black Cross Society and a "Liberation Army." On August 1, 1920, he led a march of the army, blessed by the "First Patriarch of the African Orthodox Church."

Garvey's activities made the American Negro the laughing stock of educated African Negroes in Europe. His newspaper, the *Negro World,* achieved a wide circulation among the less responsible as well as among those who thought it was a great joke. Garvey was finally discredited when he was sent to prison for using the mails to defraud. He was accused, too, of accepting money from the Ku Klux Klan to discredit the NAACP as an organization led by half-castes.

Leadership of the African Negro, after the First World War, passed to students at British and French universities, principally the universities of London and Paris.

Kwame Nkrumah (1909-   ), first president of Ghana, and until his fall from grace in 1966 the most important African leader, was educated first in America and then at the University of London. He once said that it was only by chance that French students did not dominate the independence movement. Dubois was a French-speaking Negro, with many friends in Paris, among them the Negro *deputé* for Senegal, Blaise Diagne. The French authorities were very sympathetic to the assimilated Negro who showed the proper admiration for French culture. French landladies practiced no visible discrimination against Negro students, nor did French girls. Yet the very permissiveness of the French made it easy for the Negro student to be absorbed into the French way of life and to forget that he had a duty to the people back home who needed his leadership. The French Communist Party, following Stalin's instructions, encouraged the Negro student to consider himself part of the avant garde of metropolitan France, with a special experience to contribute to home politics.

The situation in Great Britain, or rather London (where most of the West African students were) was different. The British government was vaguely committed to a program which would lead African and other colonial states toward self-government. The Colonial Office had among its civil servants many members of the Fabian Society, the left-wing intellectual group which was pledged to end colonialism as soon as possible. Official Britain made the Negro student feel at the outset that he was being trained for political responsibility back home in Africa. None of the three major parties—Labour, Liberal and Conservative—thought seriously about putting up Negro candidates in national or local elections; the average British voter would simply have voted for the other side. The notion of a Negro sitting as a member in the House of Commons was laughable.

The average Briton is inclined to discriminate against all foreigners. The African Negro student found that along with Poles, Bulgars, Hungarians and Irishmen, he was not welcome in many lodging houses, nor was there any place for him in the recreational and cultural societies organized by the British for themselves. So West African students (the most numerous of the Negroes) organized their own social life, which centered around the West African Students' Union (WASU), a club with its own residential hotel. WASU and its journal, founded in 1925, became the focal point for all independence struggles, French and British, throughout the twenties and thirties.

The founders of WASU were at first pan-African, like Dubois. They accepted his thesis that Africa would have to be liberated as a whole, that colonial frontiers were only lines drawn on a map by imperialists and were of no significance to Africans themselves. However, the leaders of WASU realized that it would be difficult to work directly with educated and progressive French Negroes, whose cultural outlook and attitude to Africa were different. And the fact that WASU was a *West* African organization abroad made it inevitable that the efforts of its leaders should be concentrated on first liberating the British colonies on the West African coast, and first and foremost the Gold Coast and Nigeria.

The British Colonial Office encouraged WASU and its leaders, and even helped in finding financial aid for WASU's publications. The general feeling at the Colonial Office was that these students, steeped in British democratic traditions at the University of London, were more likely to lead stable, pro-British governments of self-governing colonies than the chiefs at home.

The attitude of the chiefs to the de-tribalized students was one of extreme suspicion. The students were loyal to no chiefs, and acknowledged membership of no tribe. The Gold Coast Aborigines' Protection Society (GCAPS), on the other hand, encouraged participation by chiefs and loyal young Africans in various colonial government institutions. WASU disapproved of the GCAPS, as an organization likely to produce only a new generation of

Africans servile to both their British masters and their traditional tribal chiefs. The GCAPS, in fact, lost its influence after the passing of an Act in 1925 which reduced the number of nominees (chiefs or pro-chief Africans) on the Gold Coast's Legislative Council—an Act urged by WASU and its supporters in the British Colonial Office.

WASU also opposed the National Congress of West Africa, an organization inspired by the Indian leader, Mahatma Ghandi (1869-1948), which believed in achieving independence by applying non-violent pressure on the British and French colonial governments. When the time came, WASU leaders believed, violence might be necessary to break the last links in the chain which bound West Africa to Britain and France. In the meantime, the correct policy was to press for a steady increase in African representation by elected Africans with no tribal loyalties in every legislative body in the colonies. It would be up to these Africans to reform existing legislative bodies and suggest new ways of governing the colonies until eventually there would be no nominees of the governor. When this day came the governor would merely represent the Crown, and have no more power than the constitutional monarch had in Britain, or the president in pre-war France.

The cost of traveling back and forth from West Africa made it very difficult for the students in London to keep in touch with de-tribalized Africans at home. This created a curious situation. Missionaries, and the Africans they educated to pre-university standard, had their ideas of the correct pace at which the struggle for independence should proceed. WASU students, courted by the Colonial Office, were led to believe that they could more or less fix the date on which effective power would be handed over. The missionaries and their friends became convinced that there was a conspiracy afoot to make the newly-independent states, when established, godless—a conviction born of the knowledge that many of WASU's leaders were atheists, and many Colonial Office Fabians were agnostics. The net result of the isolation of WASU students and the suspicions of the missionaries was that during the thirties almost no progress was made toward independence, which very well suited the British Conservative governments of the day.

The Second World War gave a new impetus to the struggle for independence. The colonies in general were left very much to themselves as the British government in London grappled with the problems of waging the war, at first alone, then with the Soviet Union and the United States (both anti-imperialist powers) as allies. All the British government could do for West Africa was to guarantee to buy all the cocoa crop, through the Purchasing Department of the Ministry of Food. Cocoa had less far to travel than tea, and was more nutritious. Gold Coast cocoa growers became more prosperous than ever before, and had time to dabble in politics. The growers dabbled to such good effect, led by former WASU students who had come home for the war, that in 1947 they were able to insist that a Cocoa Marketing Board be set up to replace the Ministry of Food's Purchasing Department. The Board paid farmers a guaranteed price for the crop, banking the surplus during the years when the world price was high and subsidizing the growers in the lean years. Some of the surplus was transferred to a fund which was used for education and, inevitably, political education.

In 1947 and 1948 the former WASU students and the missionary-educated progressives found that they had a substantial number of supporters in the Gold Coast who had money to spend on political organization. Out of the cocoa growers and the other de-tribalized Africans in the cities, who were growing more prosperous every day, Dr. J. B. Danquah (1895-   ) forged the first African political party with roots in both town and country. He called it the United Gold Coast Convention, and he invited a former WASU student, Kwame Nkrumah, to become its director.

Nkrumah decided that the time was ripe for self-government for the Gold Coast. There was a Labour government in power in Britain pledged to grant independence to colonies which showed themselves ready for it. Nkrumah believed that "one shove and independence is ours," that a show of "forceful intention" would convince his friends in the Labour government in London that the Gold Coast was not only ready for independence but insistent on getting it immediately.

In February 1948, Nkrumah led a boycott of European goods on sale in the shops in Accra, and a march on the governor's residence. Shots were fired by the police, and rioting followed. Nkrumah and Danquah were imprisoned and a Commission of Inquiry was sent out from London to investigate. The Commission's report recognized that reforms were necessary which would bring an African majority into the government of the Gold Coast, so that long-term economic planning would be possible. A Constitutional Committee was set up in 1949, and given the task of drafting a pre-self-government charter for the colony. Danquah was all for helping this Committee; Nkrumah felt that the time for talk was past.

The two men parted political company and Nkrumah founded the Convention Peoples Party, taking with him most of the United Gold Coast Convention's funds and organizers. In January 1950, Nkrumah threatened to organize a general strike and another boycott, this time of all European-owned shops. He was jailed to prevent him from sparking off further disorders.

At this point the British government decided that if it held Nkrumah in jail long enough, the African-in-the-street would forget him, and the moderate Danquah would regain control of the independence movement. This was unjustified optimism on the part of the British government. The Constitutional Committee met, drafted and enacted a new constitution in London, then fixed the

Kwame Nkrumah (born 1909), first president of Ghana
Photo: Paul Popper

date for a general election in the Gold Coast for February 1951. When the election was held, Nkrumah's party won thirty-four of the thirty-eight seats, and Danquah's party only three (the other seat went to an independent). Nkrumah himself, though still in jail, won a seat in Accra, the capital. The governor was obliged not only to release him but to recognize him as Leader of Government Business in the new Assembly and, in March 1952, as Prime Minister.

In 1954, yet another new constitution removed from the Assembly the last member nominated by the British government, and from then on the Gold Coast was to be a parliamentary democracy. At the general election of 1954, Nkrumah's party won seventy-one of the 104 seats. The new Northern People's Party came into existence, representing the chiefs and other social, religious and intellectual minorities, and constituting an official opposition.

At this point the left-wing British politicians were satisfied. They deplored the violence Nkrumah had used, but were willing to overlook it because now there was a democratic state, with an elected parliament containing an official opposition. What well-meaning people in Britain did not understand was that the Ashanti trusted Nkrumah, a southerner, no more than the leaders of the Northern People's Party did. The Ashanti, in fact, formed their own National Liberation Movement and asked the British government (the Conservatives by this time had succeeded Labour) for separate independence, or at least equal rights with the former Gold Coast in a federal state.

The British government, Nkrumah and the leaders of the Ashanti continued their wrangling for two years.

British Conservative leaders maintained that what was sauce for the Gold Coast goose was sauce for the Ashanti gander. Why shouldn't the Ashanti have their own state? Nkrumah pointed out that if this came about, the former Northern Territories would also want autonomy, and this would "balkanize" the new state (turn it into a collection of quarreling regions, similar to the Balkan peninsula in Europe), making it economically and politically weak. In July 1956, Nkrumah's popularity and point of view were put to the test when the British half of the former German colony of Togoland went to the polls and voted to join Nkrumah's Gold Coast rather than their other fellow-tribesmen still ruled by the French. Nkrumah called a general election and put the issue to all the voters in the north, Ashanti and the Gold Coast proper. Was it to be three states or one? He won the election, gaining seventy-two seats out of 104. In March 1957, the Gold Coast, including Ashanti and Togoland, became fully independent, and took the name of Ghana.

On July 1, 1960, Ghana became a republic within the British Commonwealth, with Nkrumah as its first president.

The pattern set by WASU, the Colonial Office and Nkrumah has been followed throughout West Africa and, indeed, all over English-speaking Africa.

France was slower to encourage or even recognize the existence of an independence movement among its African subjects. As late as 1946, the new French constitution contained a clause which hinted that the drafters of the constitution still hoped for the assimilation of Africans into a greater France, ruled from Paris. Once Africans had absorbed French culture and become *"assimilés,"* they would be entitled to offer themselves as candidates for the highest offices of state. Even before World War II, a French-speaking Negro from Guiana had been governor of Chad. The British, with all their talk of progress toward self-government, could not produce a similar example of equality of opportunity before the war.

The rise to power of Kwame Nkrumah radically changed the attitude of French-speaking African Negroes to assimilation. It was quickly noted that the 1946 constitution had in fact created two classes of Frenchmen. Everybody was a member of the French Union, and France itself had no larger representation in the Union's assemblies than any other territory—representation was based only on population and not on color. But the French Chamber of Deputies, which had the real power, was in the hands of the metropolitan French who had ninety-six per cent of the seats, leaving only four per cent for Africans, Asians and other colonials. This was not good enough for the post-war French-speaking Negro.

Some of the not quite equal French citizens believed that political activity in France itself could result in a change in this situation. They joined the de Gaullist party, the RPF, or the Socialist Party, but even then found themselves regarded as second-class politicians, invited only to speak on colonial affairs. The vast majority of progressive, active Negroes joined a new party, the Rassemblement Democratiqué Africaine (RDA), which took a WASU-Nkrumah line. What was needed, said the leaders of RDA, was steady progress towards self-government, colony by colony, and no more talk of being absorbed into a multicolored France.

After Nkrumah's success in 1954, many white French politicans were afraid that the RDA would look for ways to add the territory of French colonies to that freed from the British. Former French colonies would revolt and, what was worse, end up as part of the Sterling Area, members of the British Commonwealth. In 1954, the leader of the RDA was hurriedly invited to Paris and asked to accept the portfolio of a new Ministry which would look for an alternative to Nkrumahism. The new minister, Houphouet-Boigny (1905-   ), drafted the "loi-cadre" which, by giving a certain amount of local self-government, was supposed to lay the foundations of a new French commonwealth. On June 23, 1956, each French Colony was given its own government, responsible for internal affairs. A Territorial Assembly would choose a prime minister and cabinet, and the governor would merely represent loyalty to a France responsible for defense and foreign affairs.

The loi-cadre was a large step forward, and represented a radical change in French thinking. But it came too late. Ghana's independence, which was complete by 1957, its change of name to one completely African, and Nkrumah's growing importance as a symbol of African independence made French-speaking Africans dissatisfied with their "half a cake." Houphouet-Boigny was jealous of Nkrumah's fame, though he felt that something useful could evolve from the application of the loi-cadre. Some of his friends who were politically moderate thought that a federation of equal partners, including metropolitan France, would work without seeming to slavishly imitate the British. On the left, Sékou Touré, (1922-   ), premier of Guinea and the most brilliant of the young French Negroes, maintained that there was no alternative to the Nkrumah model. Later, there could be talks about the federation of independent African states, French and English speaking, but this had to come after independence.

The coup d'état of May 1958, which restored General de Gaulle (1890-   ) to power in France, was inspired by a general dissatisfaction with the way successive governments had handled the independence problem. De Gaulle's supporters in the RDA thought that the General would find a solution, and the right, led by Houphouet-Boigny, was also hopeful. In fact, de Gaulle proposed the establishment of a "French Community," in which all states would have equal rights, though in an interim period the government in Paris would have the final say in defense and foreign affairs, advised by the premiers of the self-governing members of the Community. During the summer of 1958 he toured West Africa trying to sell his idea to the leaders of the French-speaking West African states, and seemed to be having some success until he reached Conakry, the capital of Guinea. There he found that Sékou Touré was by no means convinced that the Community was anything more than a trick to preserve French rule while pretending to grant independence to the colonies. Sékou Touré told De Gaulle flatly that he would vote against the Community, and exercise his right to work for full independence.

On October 2, 1958, Sékou Touré proclaimed the independence of the second Black African former colony, being ranked second only to Kwame Nkrumah in the list of leaders of the liberation movement. Other French-speaking Negroes criticized Guinea's action. Senghor (1906-   ), the leader of the Senegalese, said: "Poor Sékou Touré! He will never walk along the Champs Elysées again." De Gaulle reacted violently, closing all Guinea's traditional markets for bauxite and bananas (the principal exports). France's traditional allies said they would refuse to recognise the new republic, which found itself in considerable economic difficulties.

But before Christmas of 1958, Nkrumah had come to the rescue of Sékou Touré, offering a loan of ten million pounds, and union with Ghana to form the nucleus of a United States of West Africa. Nkrumah's determination to help, and Sékou Touré's determination to survive, convinced most European powers that it would be foolish to continue to ignore the new republic. British missions reported that the people of Guinea were working without pay in support of their president. A Catholic Church delegation made it clear that Sékou Touré, though a Muslim, would not practice religious discrimination, and by the end of 1959 the Republic of Guinea had been formally recognized by most of the states of the world; it was a member of the United Nations, and had weathered its economic crisis successfully.

Sékou Touré's survival meant the end of the French Community, almost before it had begun its uncertain life in West Africa. Senghor, the president of Senegal which was within the French Community, tried to form a union with the French South Saharan Sudan (Mali) in 1959, as a counterweight to Nkrumah and Sékou Touré's Guinea-Ghana union, but this was not a success. Nobody could afford to be less than Sékou Touré, and one by one the states within the French Community gave notice to de Gaulle that they would leave and claim complete independence. By the end of August 1960, Senegal, Mauritania, Mali, the Upper Volta, Niger, Chad, the Ivory Coast, Togo, Dahomey and the Cameroons were all independent and members of the United Nations.

Nkrumah and Sékou Touré were so successful that even the leaders of the moderate Nigerians decided that they could not wait for the gradual progress towards independence which was planned to end in full freedom in 1960.

Nigeria's problems were difficult to solve. The three distinct regions over which Lugard had ruled were still intact. In the Western Region, the wealthy Yoruba tribe, led by Chief Awolowo (1909-), wanted to co-operate with the British Colonial Office in a gradual development of economic and political institutions. Already, in 1949, Awolowo had seen the opening of the first University College in West Africa (Ibadan) in his Region and he was sure that the longer he waited, within limits, the wealthier would the new independent Federal State of Nigeria be when it was proclaimed. The 1946 constitution had given him control over the Regional House of Assembly—forty per cent of whose members he nominated through the tribal councils—and most of the rest of the members (nominated by the British) followed his line.

The Eastern Region of Nigeria was controlled by Azikiwe (1904-), a journalist who had welded the Ibo tribe into a National Council of Nigeria and the Cameroons (which even had some support in the Western Region). Azikiwe was impatient for independence, even before the Nkrumah-Sékou Touré "golden years," but he did not agree with Awolowo on the form and content of the constitution of an independent Nigeria. He preferred a single state, and was opposed to the idea of continuing a federation indefinitely. He enjoyed the support of the Eastern Region House of Assembly, and controlled most of the press in the federal capital of Lagos.

The Northern Region of Nigeria was ruled almost feudally by the Sardauna of Sokoto. There were no elected members in his Regional Parliament. There was a House of Chiefs, to which all the most important chiefs belonged by right, and there was a House of Assembly, whose members were selected by the governor on his advice. There was a party of sorts, the Northern Peoples Congress, founded by Alhaji Abubakar Tafawa Balewa (1912-   ), but the Sardauna and his emirs controlled this, too. An opposition party, the Northern Elements Progressive Union, largely financed by Azikiwe from the east, led a dangerous and uncertain life, its leaders murdered with monotonous regularity by "unknown persons." The Sardauna of Sokoto was in no hurry for independence. He certainly did not want to lose his own independence in a unitary state, like the one proposed by Azikiwe, and he had a sneaking feeling that he would be no match for Awolowo in an independent federal parliament.

During 1957, a conference took place in London to discuss independence and fix a date for the transfer of power. Nkrumah had become ruler of independent Ghana in the spring, and neither Awolowo nor the Sardauna of Sokoto could restrain those of their followers who insisted that 1960 was the "latest possible date" for their independence. Nobody really believed that this date was "real," and so the three strong men agreed that Abubakar Balewa should be designated the first Federal Prime Minister of the new state, if and when it was proclaimed. Azikiwe and Awolowo returned to Nigeria to continue their own campaigns aimed at consolidating their holds on their Regions.

The upset in Guinea in 1958, however, made it clear to both Azikiwe and Awolowo that they would be lucky if they could hold off their extremist followers for as long as two years. During 1959, when it became obvious that the French Community could not survive, there were riots in Lagos by young students shouting "Will we be the last to be free in West Africa?" Azikiwe began a new campaign, reminding his followers in the Eastern Region and elsewhere that he had been the first Nigerian to graduate abroad (at Lincoln College and the University of Pennsylvania in the twenties). He had been the pioneer of Nigerian popular journalism, the local antidote to *The Times*. He was, therefore, the natural choice of all progressive Nigerians as leader of any newly-independent state. Awolowo, for his part, profited from his great business acumen and experience by waging a public relations campaign the like of which Africa had never seen. He hired helicopters to drop pamphlets on villages, even where he knew that the villagers could neither read nor write. He wrote his name in the sky with the help of a French sky-writing pilot. The Sardauna of Sokoto did nothing.

As it turned out, and Nigerians said it was the way of Nigeria, none of these last minute efforts to establish the claims of Azikiwe or Awolowo had any effect. On October 1, 1960, Nigeria became independent, with Awolowo still supreme in the Western Region, Azikiwe in the Eastern Region, the Sardauna of Sokoto in the Northern, and Abubakar Balewa as Federal Prime Minister.

The other British colonies in West Africa, Gambia and Sierra Leone, could not be held back for long. Much smaller than the Gold Coast or Nigeria (together Gambia and Sierra Leone have a population of only two and one-half million), their leaders nevertheless felt that they would be swallowed up by their newly-independent neighbors (Sierra Leone by Guinea and Gambia by Senegal) if they, too, did not press the British government for a constitution and self-government.

Sierra Leone, like Liberia a settlement of freed slaves, was also similar to Liberia in that it lacked a history of democracy. Slavery was finally abolished only in 1928, and it was the freed slaves themselves who had been enslaving the native Africans. But many members of the freed slave aristocracy had studied at British universities and there was probably a higher proportion of educated Africans in the colony than in the Gold Coast. The colony was also potentially very ,wealthy, partly because good crops of rice and coffee were raised, and partly because a lot of money was made by the illegal smuggling of diamonds found in the Sewa and Rokel rivers. Sir Milton Margai (1895-   ) led a delegation of descendants of freed slaves to London, and agreed that independence should be granted in 1961 (it was, in fact, granted on April 27, 1961). The British Conservative government of the day had no doubt that Sierra Leone would continue to make progress along the road to democracy and prosperity.

Gambia, or The Gambia as it is formally known, was never more than an enclave on the River Gambia, giving formal shelter to the British merchants who began trading there (in slaves) in 1588. After the French had abandoned all claims to the river area in 1815, the Gambia continued to live an uneasy life, sometimes ruled from Sierra Leone (1821-1843, 1866-1888), sometimes as a separate colony. No attempt was made to encourage African participation in government until 1947, when a new constitution permitted native representation in the Legislative Council. In 1954, after the Gold Coast's first leap forward, another new constitution provided for an elected majority in the Executive Council which made all the important decisions (on the governor's advice). After the 1958 Sékou Touré-Nkrumah call to arms there were demonstrations in the capital of Bathurst; the British government discovered, however, that it was useless to talk of immediate independence, as from among the colony's 316,000 inhabitants it would have been difficult to find a sufficient number of Africans to form even a provisional government. Nonetheless, in May 1962, a degree of self-government was given to the colony, after an intensive training program for "officials," and in October 1963, full responsibility for internal affairs was granted. At this time there was some talk of federation with Senegal, but the language barrier proved too great, and in 1965, the colony became independent within the British Commonwealth.

Throughout all the excitement, the shouting, the crises, and the progress of the independence movement in West Africa, Liberia remained unaffected, ruled by the corrupt single party under the presidency of William Tubman (1895-   ), who was re-elected in 1963 to his twenty-first year of office. A political backwater, internationally bankrupt, the state continues to exist, thanks to the profits made by the Firestone Rubber Company, and to the extensive illegal traffic in diamonds. At the time this was written there seemed to be little likelihood that democracy or a conventional government would come to Black Africa's first independent state.

9 Spanish and Portuguese opposition to African nationalism; problem of the Belgian Congo; Belgian withdrawal and internal confusion

THE WAVE OF DEMANDS PRESENTED BY FRENCH MEMBERS of the Community in 1959 for independence in 1960 whetted the appetites of African leaders in all the other colonies on the continent. There were no exceptions. There was no question now, as far as black Africans were concerned, of any future for Africa except as a collection of states with black majority rule. Britain and France, more or less reluctantly, accepted the dissolution of their empires as inevitable. Italy, which had only Eritrea (it became a province of Ethiopia in 1962) and Somalia (which became a U.N. Trust Territory in 1950, and independent in 1960) to lose, followed the British and French line of least resistance.

There were three exceptions to the general rule that in imperial capitals all agreed that independence had to come. The Spanish government announced that it had no intention of changing the status of its colonies, which were considered provinces of the mother country. The Portuguese government had long ago declared that its colonies would continue indefinitely as provinces, too, ruled from the metropolitan capital, Lisbon. And South

Africa, independent since 1931, did not see why its empire, the territory of South West Africa, should ever be free. It should also be remembered that though most governments accepted the principle of black majority rule, British and French settlers in Algeria and East Africa did not agree. Their struggles will be discussed in a later chapter.

Between the reactionary attitude of the Spanish, Portuguese and South African governments, and the permissive attitudes of the British and French, lay the uncertainty of the Belgian government, the "proprietor" of the Congo since 1908.

Since 1925, the Congo had been ruled by three distinct administrations, only one of them directly responsible to the government in Brussels. The Roman Catholic Church looked after education, paying for schools and missions out of its own resources, although from time to time it received a subsidy from the Belgian government. The owners of commercial monopolies in the Congo ruled their railways and plantations autocratically and were only occasionally asked to report to Brussels on what they were doing. As long as they paid their taxes, they were left alone. And then there was the Belgian Colonial Civil Service, which had to account to Brussels, though the vast distance between Leopoldville and Brussels made it possible for only vague reports to be given.

Not even the most enthusiastic missionary could say in 1959 that the Church had offered to the native Congolese much in the way of education. At first it was decided that only genuine converts should be given places in mission schools. The climate of the Congo is not pleasant and missions are expensive to maintain. An unexpected consequence of this decision was the emergence of several Christian sects, violently hostile to the Catholic Church.

Perhaps the best known of these sects was that led by Kimbangu, who had come under the influence of Jehovah's Witnesses and had worked out his own version of their teachings. Kimbangu was also anti-Belgian, and was eventually arrested by the authorities for disturbing the peace. One of his disciples, Mpadi, discredited the movement by asking for Hitler's help to oust the Belgians.

The Church learned its lesson from Kimbangu, and after World War II, opened its schools to all Congolese, whether their conversion was genuine or not. Places for 500,000 in primary schools were made available and it was hoped that the majority of the Congo's 15,000,000 inhabitants would be literate by 1970. The Belgian government, however, was not very enthusiastic about the idea of a native population one day competing with Europeans for even the least responsible posts in the administration. Until 1948 the Church was forbidden to open even *one* secondary school for Africans; even after 1948, it was allowed to make places available for only 3,000. The 3,000 advanced students were supposed to be trained in the main for jobs as fitters and mechanics in the mines, jobs which were open because few Belgians were willing to work in the expanding mining industry in the Congo. Not more than 500 Congolese a year, from 1948 to 1959, had any chance of pursuing their studies with the hope of eventually entering a university. It was not until 1955 that a few Congolese were sent to Belgium to study at Polytechnics and universities.

As a contrast to the slow progress made in educating Africans for administration, the Congolese economy was intelligently developed in the interests of both Africans and Europeans. As more railways were built to ship it out, the copper in Katanga and Kasai became more and more profitable and, especially after the Second World War, became the mainstay of the economy. There was little success with the many ambitious schemes for planting coffee and bananas, but the country's timber industry prospered and the cities of Leopoldville, Elisabethville, Stanleyville, Albertville, Bukavu and Coquihatville grew apace. Leopoldville reached a population of one million in the middle fifties.

In the cities, the Africans found that there was no racial discrimination against them as Africans. Only a few had as good an education as the European administrators, but they were allowed to open their own clubs, and these became meeting places for native clerks, shopkeepers and merchants, in which further study was possible. The first political leaders of the Congolese acquired their followers in the clubs—Joseph Kasavubu (1910-   ) in Leopold-ville, Moise Tshombe (1919-   ) in Elisabethville, Antoine Gizenga (1925-   ) and Patrice Lumumba (1925-1961) in the east. Encouraged by the Jesuits, these enlightened Congolese pressed for reforms which would make possible the establishment of multiracial univer-sities in Leopoldville and Elisabethville.

In the middle fifties, however, there was a sudden hardening of Belgian government opinion about the wisdom of allowing reform-minded Congolese to nourish fantastic dreams of university education and even-tual participation in government. At first the Congo-lese did not react violently. They believed that in a little while the Belgian government would change, and then things would be as they had been before. In any event, the only nationally known leader in the Congo, Lumumba, was arrested in 1956 for embezzling funds from the post office where he worked as a clerk, and sentenced to two years imprisonment. The other strong leaders in the different regions had not decided what they wanted for an independent Congo, always supposing that this was possible. Kasavubu and Tshombe favored, if anything, splitting up the Congo with independence for the various regions, each one with its dominant tribe. In any event, until 1958, all was quiet in the clubs.

Discussion about independence between the Belgian government and the leaders of the Congolese began more or less by accident. In 1958, the government decided to have a Congo Pavilion at the Brussels World Fair. Congolese were flown to the Belgian capital to set up the Pavilion, which was supposed to show the happy life of the natives under Belgian administration. There were schools at work and villages at play for visitors to see, and even a club in session. However, as the World Fair attracted more and more visitors, the Congolese in charge of the Pavilion began to meet European liberals and even African, including Ghanaian, politicians who accused the Congolese of being timid lackeys of colonialism. They were urged to tell the Belgian government that they would only keep the Pavilion open if it were made into something more than a sort of zoo. The government closed the Pavilion during the discussions with its Congolese attendants, and the discussions soon came around to the subject of independence, or at least equal partnership with the Europeans in the Congo.

When the Congolese leaders returned from Brussels they were met by an angry Lumumba, released from jail, who accused them of having made the Congolese the laughing stock of Black Africa. Lumumba had not only found himself a well-paid job as salesman for a beer firm, but had also convinced the editors of the two native

Congolese newspapers, *Conscience Africaine* and *Présence Congolaise,* that he was the natural leader of the Congolese and the only man the Belgians feared. He alleged that his imprisonment for embezzlement had been "an imperialist plot." And he was believed. He had attended the All-African Peoples Congress in Accra and had convinced both Nkrumah and Sékou Touré that he represented a resurgent Congo.

A few days after Lumumba's denunciation of the "timid lackeys of imperialism," his rival Kasavubu organized a series of demonstrations in Leopoldville which degenerated into riots. Kasavubu himself insisted that he had instructed his party, Alliance des Ba-Kongo, or **ABAKO**, to make only "dignified protest," and accused Lumumba of having fomented disturbances. The riots continued and more than one hundred people were killed.

The governments in Brussels and in Leopoldville panicked. The Leopoldville government under Van Hemelrijck tried to enforce law and order by imprisoning all the Congolese politicians it could lay hands on. European settlers, mostly Belgian, organized a militia to defend their lives and property. Then the government in Brussels, through a speech by King Baudouin (1936-   ), turned about-face and announced concessions to the Congolese "liberators," which included a general election by universal suffrage before the end of the year, and the convening of a Congolese native parliament in 1960.

There was chaos and consternation in the Congo. Belgian settlers either prepared to leave, or threatened to fight any attempt to "force the natural rate of progress of the native." The more moderate of the settlers pointed out that there were only sixteen native university graduates; yet the convocation of a native parliament would mean that the civil service would automatically become Congolese. Kasavubu, who had been imprisoned and exiled under the emergency regulations, returned in triumph to excite still more panic. Van Hemelrijck resigned in September 1959, and the new Governor-general, De Schrijver, immediately took the side of the moderate settlers and tried to persuade Lumumba and Kasavubu that the precipitate granting of independence and self-government would mean playing into the hands of irresponsible, often illiterate, extremists. Kasavubu, who respected De Schrijver as a man who understood the Congo and its problems, was inclined to favor putting on the brake a bit, but Lumumba said "one good push and independence is ours," and carried the day. A state of emergency was declared and all disorders repressed with some viciousness by the security forces.

But at the end of 1959, De Schrijver was forced to call for local elections throughout the Congo, implementing the king's proclamation. The settlers waited to see if the more moderate Kasavubu or the hothead Lumumba would emerge victorious. It was thought that their parties, the ABAKO and the Mouvement National Congolais, were the only serious contestants.

However, when the election results were declared, there was uproar. The majority of the seats on local councils, nationwide, had been won by the Parti Nationale du Progrès (PNP), a hitherto almost unknown organization. Investigation quickly showed that the PNP had been organized, financed, and supported even at the ballot box by the European settlers and government officials. Even so, Lumumba and his allies, and Tshombe, leader of the Katanga Congolese, had managed to win control of their regional government institutions. There were riots again, and once more the security forces repressed them, often with unnecessary violence.

After the elections, the Belgian government panicked again. It was as if the majority of politicians in Belgium wanted to wash their hands of the Congo completely. They had inherited the colony from King Leopold and he had left them only a testament of trouble. The Belgian people as a whole had not benefited from this colonial possession. Socialists said that the profits made by owners of monopoly concessions, that were spent in Belgium, had only made the class struggle more bitter. Now the Congolese themselves wanted their independence. Well, let them have it. This, at any rate, was the impression De Schrijver had of opinion at home, and he felt nervous, having arrested Lumumba, who day by day was becoming the accepted leader of the independence movement.

In January 1960, the Belgian government called a meeting of Congolese leaders in Brussels. Notwithstanding the fact that the PNP had been proved a "settlers private plot," its representatives were given prominence at the meeting. Chiefs who were thought to be loyal to Belgium were also well represented. In all, sixty-two of the eighty-one delegates were handpicked because of their loyalty. It was a shock and an unpleasant surprise for the Belgian government when they were presented with a unanimous resolution calling for independence by June 1960. "Loyalists" had been frightened out of their wits by Lumumba, who had shown them the scars of beatings he had received in Belgian prisons and had promised even worse beatings for any "loyalists" who did not support him.

The Belgian government was advised by De Schrijver and others that it had no alternative but to grant

Boys of the Congolese Junior Red Cross marshal
younger children who are collecting milk distributed
by the United Nations. A scene from Leopoldville in
1960 *Photo: Associated Press.*

Katanga's boy army. A boy with a home-made "rifle"
in a parade in the native quarter of Elizabethville in
1961 *Photo: Associated Press*

Lumumba's demands. Independence Day was set for June 30, 1960, with a general election to be held in May to decide the complexion of the first independent government.

Of all the countries of Africa, the Congo was perhaps the least prepared for independence. Politicians in neighboring Portuguese Angola pointed this out. There were few Africans qualified or experienced enough to man a government or staff a civil service. The senior posts in industry, commerce, and hospital and educational services were all held by Europeans, mostly Belgians, and many of them seemed to be ready to flee the Congo as soon as independence was a fact. Worse, the Belgian government did not seem to understand that, as in the case of Nigeria, only a federal state stood any chance of survival; the Brussels Conference, bowing to pressure from Lumumba, opted for a strong central government for the Congo. Not even the results of the May elections seemed to drive this point home. Lumumba won only thirty-three out of the 137 seats allocated to the central parliament. In the capital, Leopoldville, and the Lower Congo, Kasavubu's ABAKO won twenty-two seats, and in Katanga, Tshombe won a majority of seats in direct competition with a party pledged to support Lumumba. As it was, Lumumba was only able to form a government by setting up a coalition government which tried to placate the various regional parties, making Kasavubu president of the new Republic of the Congo.

Throughout the later stages of the struggle for independence, the Congolese leaders had the counsel not only of well-meaning (and not so well-meaning) Europeans, but also of Nkrumah and Sékou Touré. All stressed the importance of having plans for economic development and political education ready for "the Day." Sékou Touré pointed out the French saying that it is "easy to get a husband, harder to keep him," drawing the parallel that in the present political climate of Africa and Europe it was "easy to get independence, harder to make it work." Yet even before the formal proclamation of independence on June 30, 1960, well-meaning people were having difficulty in working out for themselves who represented the real power in the Congo. Lumumba was prime minister designate, but was obviously an unstable character, supported only by a minority in the east. Tshombe, though in control in Katanga, the richest region, was supported by many settlers and therefore was suspect as possibly being in their pay. Kasavubu was strong and wise, yet he had surrendered to Lumumba and taken the ceremonial post of Head of State. The other leaders—Cyrille Adoula, Albert Kalonji (1929-   ), Joseph Ileo (1922-   ), and Joseph Mobutu(1930-   )—were unknown quantities. Not even the Catholic Church, with its three archbishops, eleven African bishops and (they claimed) six million converts, could offer any definite advice, though Pope John XXIII (1881-1963) asked for detailed reports and recommendations. Protestant missions, which had infiltrated the Congo bordering on British East Africa and claimed one million converts, predicted "chaos, confusion, murder and maladministration." Events over the next few years were to prove them right.

I O
The situation in Algeria; Algeria's struggle for independence; the Mahgreb independent; Ethiopia and Eritrea independent; Somalia independent

THE CHAOS AND CONFUSION, AND SUBSEQUENT BLOODSHED, which followed the granting of independence to the former Belgian Congo, horrified and distressed many people. There was another, more unfortunate, consequence. Opinion in London and Paris hardened against the idea of giving the remaining British and French colonies their independence without absolute certainty that the colonies were ready to go it alone. In the case of British East Africa and Algeria, a large white settler population, frightened by events in the Congo, brought pressure to bear on their home governments to slow down the dissolution of the empire. The settlers in West Africa had been few in number, and so had had little say in the negotiations with African colonial leaders. In East Africa and Algeria, and in independent South Africa, the voice of the white population came through loud and clear.

The situation in Algeria was very complicated. By the end of 1960, Algeria was the only country in North Africa which had not achieved independence. Egypt had been independent since 1922, and the Sudan since 1956. Libya had been independent since 1951, and Algeria's neighbors,

Tunisia and Morocco, like the Sudan, had been on their own since 1956. Pressure from Tunisia and Morocco on both the French government and the Algerian native politicians was especially great because the three North African countries together form the Mahgreb, an area with a single heritage of custom and civilization, and there was even a movement devoted to the re-creation of a single Mahgreb community. To the south of Algeria, the French-speaking states of Mali and Niger gloated over their neighbor's political backwardness.

Yet General de Gaulle could do little, it seemed, to relieve the pressures on native Algerian politicians. A revolt of the army colonels in 1958 had brought de Gaulle himself back to power, and at least two leaders of the revolt had gone on record as saying that they would fight to the death rather than be run out of Algeria. It was not only a part of France, just across the Mediterranean. It was home for hundreds of thousands of Frenchmen. France had been chased out of Indo-China in 1954, had lost most of Africa in 1960. The time had come to call a halt. There was also another, economic consideration. In 1954 oil had been discovered in the Sahara, and France's economy had come to life after a period of postwar stagnation in the certainty that soon cheap, unlimited power would be available. De Gaulle himself saw Sahara oil as not only a source of wealth for France, but as a key to breaking "the shackles of American domination." Independent of Texas, he would also be independent of Washington.

But if General de Gaulle and the settlers were interested in preserving the status quo in Algeria, the Soviet Union and the Peoples Republic of China were very much interested in changing it. Among the leaders of the

Algerians there were probably more Communist sympathizers than anywhere else in Africa. A Communist-led state on the Mediterranean would be a very reliable and useful ally, reasoned the men in Moscow's and Peking's Africa bureaus. In 1959 the Algerians had been encouraged to form their own provisional government, promptly recognized in Peking as the lawful government and supplied with funds. At the Pan-African Congress in Tunis in February 1960, a call to arms had gone out to all African states already independent or promised independence. An African Liberation Army was to be recruited, which would "sweep the white man into the sea." The Algerian National Liberation Front wisely did not rely on the African Liberation Army, but set to work during 1960 to organize an army of its own, financed and supplied with arms by Communist China and the Soviet Union.

By the end of 1960, the National Liberation Front and provisional government in Algeria were at war with France. In vain de Gaulle promised greater autonomy for the provinces of France into which Algeria was divided. In vain he offered to extend French citizenship to all Algerians. Certain Algerian Muslims already enjoyed this privilege and had done so since 1944. By the summer of 1961 it was obvious that some concessions would have to be made to the desire for complete independence, concessions which would safeguard France's oil interests, if possible, and her right to test nuclear devices in the Sahara Desert.

But though de Gaulle, by the summer of 1961, was ready to make concessions, these were acceptable to nobody. The Algerian provisional government insisted on complete evacuation by the French. Extremists even insisted that every Frenchman, even if his family had lived in Algeria for three generations, should leave the country. At the other extreme, right-wing Frenchmen insisted that de Gaulle make no concessions. Algeria was French, and would remain French. Extremists on both sides decided to begin a campaign of terrorism and assassination which would stiffen de Gaulle's spine. Paris, once Europe's most attractive tourist city, became an armed camp. Every night there were incidents of bombings. There were three attempts on the life of the French president in the capital, and thousands of policemen and Algerian nationalists were killed or wounded. In Algeria itself, terrorism was the rule. Nationalists killed or wounded many civilians, officially by mistake. French paratroopers and Foreign Legionaries killed, wounded, and tortured to defend French Algeria. Commerce came to a virtual standstill. Worse, for the sensitive de Gaulle, world opinion turned against France as more and more cases of French Army cruelty and torture came to light.

It was probably as much due to de Gaulle's skill as to the violence of the struggle itself, that peace was restored to Algeria. By the end of 1961, de Gaulle had succeeded in convincing at least some members of the Algerian provisional government that the longer they fought, the more they would find themselves in debt to the Communists who financed and armed their Liberation Army. Would it be any different from bondage to France, this bondage to China or Moscow which might result? There was no official contact between the French and provisional Algerian governments, but unofficial contact was kept up through mutual friends in Switzerland. By the end of 1961, too, de Gaulle had succeeded in convincing his own people that the war could not go on indefinitely—raising

A French soldier on guard above
Algiers in 1962 *Photo: Associated
Press*

Street fighting in Algiers in 1960
Photo: Associated Press

taxes, lowering the standard of living in metropolitan France and keeping half a million French troops on garrison duty across the Mediterranean. In March 1962, the first official meetings between de Gaulle's representatives and the rebels took place in Evian in Switzerland and a cease fire was arranged. July 2, 1962, was named as the date for independence. The date was kept, and magically, trouble ceased. North Africa was free, except for the enclaves of Spanish Sahara and Ifni, impoverished and without either a strong desire or the resources to exist independently of Spain.

One man, perhaps, would not have agreed that the granting of independence to Algeria freed the whole of non-Negro Africa. Haile Selassie, emperor of Ethiopia, had returned to his country in 1941 after his flight from the Italians in 1936. His ambition was to restore his own personal power, and regain Eritrea and Somalia, both Italian colonies which he claimed had been stolen from Ethiopia in the nineteenth century. He did not fulfill his ambition. With the help of British troops he was restored to his throne and began to rule again autocratically, overlooking the fact that times had changed. At first he refused to have any sort of elected parliament, maintaining that as he knew all the good and able men in his country, elections would be a waste of time and money. By 1957, however, internal unrest had converted him to the notion that elections were a contemporary phenomenon, and could not be ignored. After 1957, members of the Lower House were elected, though members of the Senate were still appointed by the emperor. When, in December 1960, there was a revolt against the person and opinions of the emperor, he was forced to reorganize his entire administration and turn his attention to the second part of his ambition, the reconsolidation of the oldest empire in Africa.

Eritrea had become independent in 1952, and though Haile Selassie had tried to persuade Italy and her conquerers that it should be handed over to Ethiopia, the most he could get was an association of Ethiopia with Eritrea in a federation. He was supposed to help his smaller neighbor perfect a system of government, help it to stand on its feet—then the federation would be dissolved and both countries would be equal and independent allies. Actually nothing was done to make Eritrea a workable unit, economically or politically, and in 1962, the Eritreans confessed that they could not manage alone. Haile Selassie promptly dissolved the federation and made Eritrea a province of his empire.

Somalia was not quite so easy to "liberate from itself." The Republic of Somalia, independent in 1960, was formed of British and Italian Somaliland, united to make the new country larger and more workable. As early as 1950, when Italian Somaliland had become a U.N. Trust Territory, Haile Selassie had protested that it belonged to Ethiopia. By producing a succession of maps, not many of which were authentic, he succeeded in taking into Ethiopia the province of Ogaden, but this was the limit of his success. The new Republic of Somalia, smarting at the memory of the loss of Ogaden, was determined to keep the rest of its territory intact. The country is not poor in resources, and though eighty per cent of the population depends on the raising of cattle and the export of hides for a living, there are large deposits of high-quality iron ore. The Somalis themselves are a proud people, convinced that they are superior to every other sort of African, and are certainly good soldiers. Their attitude to Ethiopia quickly became one of actively hostile mistrust, and fighting broke out along the Somalia-Ethiopia borders. Though accused by Haile Selassie of being virtually a colony in the pay of former imperialists, Somalia survives; according to her politicians, her success in resisting Ethiopia is evidence that North Africa is now really free and can stay free.

The position in East Africa; Tanganyika's independence; the problems in Uganda; difficulties in Kenya; the Kikuyu; Mau Mau; independence gained

BRITISH EAST AFRICA WAS TO BE THE SCENE OF THE struggle for independence of the last of the sizeable colonies. It is tragic that although British West Africa made the transition to independence with relative ease and without hatred for the former conquerors, in the east there was bloodshed, murder and a generation of ill will which still plagues this part of the continent.

At first, nobody believed that things could go quite so badly. Tanganyika, in fact, made slow but steady progress toward independence. After the defeat of Germany in the First World War, it was ruled by Britain under a League of Nations mandate. From 1918 to 1925 the first British governor, Sir Horace Byatt (1875-1933), worked hard to gain the confidence of the natives. He dispossessed German settlers and gave the land back to the Africans, helping them to farm it more efficiently. Plantations of sisal, tobacco, cotton, coffee and sugar flourished; herds of cattle improved, and a start was made on the proper mapping of the country's mineral resources which include diamonds, gold, copper and silver. Byatt's successor, Sir Donald Cameron (1872-1948), was just as able.

Inheriting a colony restored to self-sufficiency, Cameron rebuilt and improved the railway system, and began to train the tribes (Sukuma, Nyamwezi, Ha, Makonde, Gogo, Haya and Chagga) for eventual self-government.

Sir Donald Cameron believed that the first step was to conduct a poll of tribal leaders, to find those whom the tribes trusted and respected. These chiefs were then given training in the administration of justice, in accountancy and in economics, and as soon as Cameron felt they were sufficiently prepared he handed over to them the whole of the administration of their tribal areas, trusting them to be just and to collect taxes honestly. In 1945 the Legislative Council was reformed, with equal representation for Europeans, Africans and the immigrant Indians. In 1946, the British government spent $100,000,000 to build a new port and railways to develop the growing of ground nuts, a project which was a failure but which did create goodwill among the native Tanganyikans who could not complain of any lack of interest in their welfare and economic progress.

In 1948, there was talk of a federation of Kenya, Uganda and Tanganyika, and an East African High Commission was set up to lay the foundations for such a federation. Like the ground nuts scheme, the project came to nothing. The Asians in East Africa were not hostile to it, but the white settlers, especially in Kenya, sabotaged the work of a Royal Commission (1953-1955) which was supposed to solve all the problems connected with the project. In 1955, therefore, Tanganyika was given a new constitution of its own and the first general election took place in 1958.

The 1955 constitution was a serious attempt to give legal form to a multiracial society. The right to vote was given to the vast majority of the population, regardless of color, and each elector had three votes which he was to cast for an African, an Asian and a European. In this way it was hoped to have an assembly which was not only multiracial but was chosen multiracially.

Victory at the elections went to the oldest party, the Tanganyika African National Union. There was some disappointment at the failure of the United Tanganyika Party, led by Europeans and blessed by the Colonial Office, but the leader of TANU, Julius Nyerere (1921-   ), was well liked. A quiet Roman Catholic teacher, he seemed to be a very satisfactory contrast to Nkrumah in West Africa. In 1960 a further general election was held, and Nyerere's party won every seat in the legislative assembly but one. On May 1, 1961, Tanganyika was given complete control over internal affairs, and on December 9, complete independence.

It all seemed to be a model of peaceful transition to self-government, during a year in which fighting in Algeria reached its bloodiest, and the condition of the Congo was alarming the whole world.

Uganda's passage to independence was stormier. There had been quarrels between the Baganda and the other tribes, and even inside the Baganda. The Parliament or Lukiiko was really not representative of the majority of the Baganda, representing in fact only the chiefs who had been given one square mile of land apiece by the 1900 agreement with Great Britain. As Buganda became more and more prosperous with the rise in world cotton prices, the differences between the standard of living of the rich and poor became more and more obvious. A new class of Africans, educated at Buganda's own technical schools and University College, began to challenge the chiefs' traditional right to rule. Leaders of the co-operative movement, too, felt they ought to have a voice in government. In 1945 there were strikes and demonstrations, and the chief minister was assassinated on the steps of the cathedral.

In 1946, a sincere attempt was made to reform the government of Buganda, and to strengthen political forces in other parts of Uganda, overshadowed by Buganda with its wealthy chiefs and well established institutions. The Lukiiko was made partially elective, just under half the seats being opened to members of the new rich peasant and intellectual classes. In the western and eastern provinces, programs for political education were drafted and two Africans from these provinces were nominated to the Legislative Council.

In 1948, this reform was seen to be insufficient. The Bataka, traditional managers of burial grounds dispossessed by the 1900 agreement, rioted. African cotton growers and clerks joined in, presenting the Kabaka with a demand for a fully elective Lukiiko, which would have control over the marketing of cotton which was now in Indian hands. The British government advised the Kabaka to grant the demand, but he was reluctant to make the Lukiiko an elected assembly. In the end the British government insisted, and though the Kabaka juggled with the constituencies so that certain chiefs were sure to be returned, he complied. The British government also set up a Marketing Board which reformed the marketing of cotton and its processing. Elected provincial councils were set up all over Uganda, and for the first time a central government began to rival the Kabaka of Buganda in wealth and power. In 1952, the central government increased its popular appeal by selling cotton gins and markets belonging to the Board to a wide range of African co-operatives. Two Uganda parties were formed, both determined to abolish the federal system and create a strong, unified state of Uganda.

In 1953, the leaders of these two parties found their first legitimate excuse for complaint against the British government. The parties had found it difficult to work up any anti-British feeling, because the protectorate had had a succession of wise and sympathetic governors. The enemy of the nationalists had always been the Kabaka who, they believed, tried to give the Baganda tribe a permanently privileged position. However, although the nationalists disliked the Kabaka, they decided to use his banishment as an excuse to rally support for the independence movement, in Buganda as well as in the eastern and western provinces.

For two years there were disputes and angry scenes at various meetings with the governor, with Sir Keith Hancock (1898-   ), sent out from London to negotiate with the nationalists, and with Dr. Ralph Bunche (1904-   ), who was asked to mediate. The British governor pointed out that the nationalists ought to support him in banishing the Kabaka, because the Kabaka had asked the Foreign Office to take Buganda out of the Federated Protectorate and grant it independence alone. But the leaders of the Uganda People's Congress (a largely Protestant party) and the Uganda National Congress (a Catholic party) set logic aside. In the end the Kabaka was allowed to return and a new constitution made Uganda a single state, though re-throning him as constitutional monarch of Buganda, an integral part of Uganda.

In 1958, the first Uganda-wide elections were held,

and in March 1961 a general election, intended to make it possible to form an all-African Ugandan government. At the 1961 election, the Uganda People's Congress had a large majority in the western and eastern provinces, and the Uganda Democratic Party the majority in Buganda. The Uganda National Congress was largely destroyed because Catholic Baganda took notice of the Kabaka's decree that they were not to vote. The Kabaka also made yet another attempt to take Buganda out of the unitary state of Uganda. The attempt failed, and Uganda became independent on October 9, 1962, with Dr. Milton Obote (1926-   ) as prime minister. What little tension there had been between the British government and the Ugandans disappeared, leaving only a continuing tension between the central government under Dr. Obote, and the "sub-state" of Buganda, ruled by the Kabaka.

British settlers in Kenya watched the progress of Tanganyika and Uganda towards independence with a mixture of envy and relief. At least they would not have an actively hostile pair of African governments on their frontiers as they fought to "save Kenya from the folly of independence and black majority rule." But there was little else to console the settlers. All over Africa natives unfit to rule had seized power and the European settlers in Algeria were being squeezed out of their homes.

Trouble in Kenya began even before the troubles in Algeria. From 1920 to 1939, considerable numbers of settlers, many with a great deal of capital, moved into the Kenya Highlands (from 1920 a colony separate from the protectorate along the coast). Some of the settlers were veterans of World War I, who were later to say that they had fought to get into Kenya and would fight to stay. Others were wealthy men like Lord Delamere who believed that Europe was going to the dogs, and only Africa could offer a gentleman a decent standard of living. Economic progress in Kenya was rapid and consistent between the wars. Coffee, tea and cotton plantations prospered, and light industries were established in and around Nairobi, the capital.

At first, a great deal of trouble was taken to involve native Kenyans in industrial and agricultural progress. Co-operatives were formed, and tribesmen were taught how to farm using modern methods. However, as early as 1922 the Kikuyu tribe formed its own Central Association pledged to dislodge the European settler from the

Houses on a tea plantation in Kenya
Photo: J. Allan Cash

Kenya : an agricultural adviser on an African cooperative farm, formerly European
Photo: J. Allan Cash

Cattle on another farm taken over by Africans after independence
Photo: J. Allan Cash

fertile Highlands "stolen from the Kikuyu." Instead of working on the European-owned plantations, where Africans were paid a high wage (by African standards) and often given land of their own, the Kikuyu preferred to migrate to Nairobi and carry on with their agitation there.

As early as 1923, a British Government Commission offered to organize elections for the Legislative Council on a single electoral roll. Europeans, Africans and Indians, if they were literate, would have equal rights as electors. The European settlers opposed this plan, pointing out that the Kikuyu were not ready to co-operate even in the interests of Kenya as a whole, but had one idea fixed in their heads, to get the European out. In 1927 a new constitution gave representation in the Legislative Council to eleven Europeans, five Indians, one Arab, and a European spokesman for the Africans, who were still not considered fit to speak for themselves. If the Kikuyu had not continued with their program of riot and protests, they would certainly have taken their place in the council under this new constitution.

The attitude of the settlers to the Kikuyu and their Central Association varied from anger to disappointment. The tribe was the most intelligent of the Bantu in Kenya, and took to modernization faster than tribes belonging to the other three groups (Nilotics, Nilo-Hamitics, and Hamitics). Kikuyu claims to all the land in the Highlands were absurd. Even before the building of the Kenya-Uganda railway had displaced them, bringing the diseases which had decimated them, Kikuyu did not occupy all the Highlands and the land on which they had been settled had been badly farmed. The European settlers in general were willing to discuss the placing of educated Kikuyu, with adequate farm training, on farms in the Highlands, but they could not accept a claim which would dislodge every European. Nor could Europeans who had invested millions of pounds in making the Highlands prosperous, even inventing the strains of wheat which grew there to feed the Kikuyu, accept the idea of land being badly farmed near their plantations and estates. The Kikuyu Land Inquiry Commission in 1929 found, further, that many individual Kikuyu claims had been bought in the streets of Nairobi, something which was contrary to tribal custom as well as to British colonial government law.

In 1932, the colonial government made a compromise which, it was hoped, would satisfy at least some of the Kikuyu. A restriction was placed on the expansion of European settlement in the Highlands, and large native reserves were created where Kikuyu could buy land and settle. Unfortunately for the Kikuyu, they were mistrusted by other tribes because so many of them had been de-tribalized and had gone to live with whites in the cities. Kikuyu found that they were unwelcome on the land, and, as economic conditions grew difficult during the thirties, they faced unemployment in the cities. Had it not been for the outbreak of the Second World War, there would certainly have been widespread chaos and bloodshed in Kenya.

World War II postponed the settlement of the landless Kikuyu. War conditions created jobs for them, and many were recruited into the Colonial Army. Friction between settlers and natives disappeared while they fought the common German enemy. Kenya Africans under British influence became even more patriotic than Tanganyika Africans, who retained some affection for the Germany of pre-1914.

However, after 1945, the crisis of the thirties became even more acute. The Kikuyu who had served in the army had stolen arms and ammunition throughout their period of service, in preparation for an armed rebellion should it be necessary. The European settlers had also secreted arms and ammunition, "to defend our rights," and had been strengthened by a new immigration of British people alarmed by the election of a socialist government in Britain itself. An attempt made in 1948 to placate African opinion by naming four Africans to the Legislative Council was rejected as absurd by the Kikuyu. It was only a matter of time before trouble broke out.

The leader of the Kikuyu, and the man later accused of being responsible for a virtual civil war, was Jomo Kenyatta (1893?-   ), principal of the Kenya Teachers' College. He was educated at a Scots Presbyterian mission school. After a year as a houseboy for a farmer, Kenyatta went to England, where he stayed until 1946. In London he met Nkrumah and worked with him and WASU, planning independence for Africa, and on his return to Kenya he became the most respected of the de-tribalized Kikuyu. Almost certainly he disapproved of the violence which was to last from 1949 until 1960—the Mau Mau terrorism—which at one time threatened to tie down as many British security forces as did the Algerian FLN in their homeland.

Much has been written about the Mau Mau, most of it inaccurate. In the beginning, when the first oaths were taken (1948-1949) it was probably little more than a secret society which aimed to unite the Kikuyu on the reserves with the Kikuyu in the towns—a purely tribal, family affair. At this stage, Kenyatta was probably sympathetic at least to the aims of the movement, though as a sophis-

Jomo Kenyatta, President of the Republic of Kenya
since 1964 *Photo: courtesy Kenya High Commission*

ticated politician he must have found the oaths and the initiation ceremonies both primitive and disgusting. He probably disapproved of the way in which different pressure groups got hold of parts of the movement and tried to make it serve their own ends. Anti-Christians were prominent in some areas, anti-whites in others. Month by month, Mau Mau became more and more violent. Land-hungry Kikuyu began to attack European farms in the Highlands, in an attempt to frighten the farmers into abandoning their homes. Anti-Christian Mau Mau attacked churches and mosques.

By the beginning of 1952, terrorism had reached such a peak that Europeans were afraid to move about without a gun. A state of emergency was proclaimed, and an attempt was made to trace Mau Mau leaders. Thought to be one of the leaders, Kenyatta was banished to northern Kenya for an indefinite period. Investigations soon confirmed that the movement was really confined to the Kikuyu, and the British colonial government tried hard to win over members of other tribes who were being terrorized and terrified by the Mau Mau. Kikuyu numbering some 90,000 were deported from Nairobi, and their places taken by members of the Luo tribe. By the end of the emergency in 1955, the Kikuyu had lost their position as the natural leaders of the African, though Kenyatta, in exile, had become something of a folk hero.

After 1955, the independence movement in Kenya was led by Tom Mboya (1936-   ) and his Kenya Independence Movement (later the Kenya African National Union). Mboya, a young Luo trade unionist, was under suspicion as a terrorist but none of the accusations against him were ever proved. He was restricted to Nairobi, which suited him well enough because he could work there among his own tribe.

In 1957, a new constitution fixed representation in the Legislative Council at fourteen Africans, fourteen Europeans and eight Asians, plus four members from each race chosen by the Council in session. The British government's argument in favor of this constitution was that self-government was inevitable one day, and it was necessary to give Africans and Asians experience in administration. Europeans relied on the fact that Asians had suffered just as much as Europeans during the Mau Mau emergency to give them a majority when important decisions were to be taken, and this, in fact, happened. The African members walked out of the Council in 1959 and did not return.

In 1960 there was another Constitutional Conference, and elections were fixed for February 1961. Mboya still led African political opinion, though there was some support for moderates from tribes other than the Kikuyu and Luo. At the elections, Mboya won a large majority, winning more seats than the only serious African rival, the Kenya African Democratic Union, and the tiny white-led New Kenya Party. Mboya then demanded the release of Jomo Kenyatta so that he could "lead his people to final and complete independence."

For two years there was a great deal of political infighting in Kenya. The European settlers, during 1962, saw the state of Algeria fall to the natives. Some of the settlers tried hard to make the Conservative government in London delay independence indefinitely. Others wanted the delay to be at least long enough to enable them to sell their properties without losing too much money. The first European refugees fled either south to the Rhodesias, or home to Britain, and there was some African terrorist pressure put on others to follow. The subtler politicians among the Europeans tried to encourage quarrels between the main African parties, KANU and KADU. They hinted to the Luo that their leader Mboya would be "given the chop" when the Kikuyu Kenyatta came back from exile and took over the leadership of the Kenyan government. Luo would be massacred or, at the very least, expelled from Nairobi. Hints were dropped to the Kikuyu that Mboya really had no intention of handing over the leadership of KANU to Kenyatta, that their Jomo would rot in exile under Mboya as he had done under white rule.

But the threat of a new terrorism, a revival of Mau Mau, and the attempts to encourage divisions among the Africans could not halt the rush towards complete independence. In May 1963, new elections were held to determine the composition of the first independent government, and KANU won sixty-four out of 112 seats to KADO's thirty-two. An African People's Party, which won eight seats, later merged with KADU, but there was no doubting who would one day become Kenya's first prime minister. Jomo Kenyatta was released, and became prime minister of Kenya on December 12, 1963. Four days later the international community recognized the state as the 113th member of the United Nations. The flight south of the last-ditch Europeans began, determined to make their stand in Southern Rhodesia, to "stick it out or die."

I 2 *Rhodesia and Nyasaland between World War I and World War II; federation of Rhodesia and Nyasaland 1953; federation dissolved 1961-6; Malawi and Zambia independent 1964; Rhodesia's Unilateral Declaration of Independence 1965*

THE BRITISH SOUTH AFRICA COMPANY'S TERRITORIES—Nyasaland, Northern and Southern Rhodesia—had been designated in the mind of Cecil Rhodes as the ideal settlement for men and women of British stock who would extend Anglo-Saxon civilization as far north as the Belgian Congo and German East Africa (Tanganyika) permitted. Settlement was not a missionary enterprise. Nobody set out to heal and convert the natives, dragging in commercial interests and governments when trouble began. Rhodes had a dream, much like the dream of the American Pilgrim Fathers, and cared as little for the indigenous people as they had. He was personally kind to natives and inspired their admiration and affection. If he thought about their future at all, it was to think them lucky to be subjects of the British Crown and to be able to live among British people.

Such a settlement philosophy was not in any way promising as a point from which to start preparing a campaign for black majority rule. Nyasaland, a British protectorate since 1892, was the only one of the three territories controlled by the British South Africa Company to enter the twentieth century with any prospect of preparation for native self-government. It was joined in 1924 by Northern Rhodesia. Southern Rhodesia, rejecting federation with South Africa in 1922, became self-governing under a white Rhodesian government in 1923. Nyasaland and Northern Rhodesia were to follow the trail blazed by Nkrumah and Colonial Office Fabians. Southern Rhodesia was to go its own way.

In the light of subsequent developments, it is important to stress that Southern Rhodesia rejected the idea of federation with South Africa by a large majority. The first overtures to Southern Rhodesia had been made before the Union of South Africa in 1910. Rhodesians, when they were at all political, except in loyalty to the British Crown, were attracted by General Smuts' theory of "Holism"—each race in a country was to develop separately, retaining its own cultural traditions, but would be loyal to the country as a whole. But Smuts was not the only South African politician. Hertzog wanted the Boer character of South Africa to be stressed in all the Union's institutions and the speaking of Afrikaans to be compulsory. Rhodesians were alarmed at the thought that their own British cultural traditions might be swamped by the Boers if they associated too closely with the richer Union. Rhodesians also mistrusted the Reds, the South African Labour Party and the Communists (who set up a Red Republic in the Rand in 1922). But Rhodesian feelings were vaguer than any particular objection to any particular aspect of the South African way of life. The average Rhodesian felt that he was closer to the Englishman at home than to the South African at the Cape. Most Rhodesians were relieved when the Union became independent as a Dominion in 1931. There was to be no further pressure on them to join the Union until the tide of African nationalism began to sweep down the east coast.

Nyasaland, before the First World War, became prosperous through the development of tea, coffee and tobacco plantations. Many Nyasas acquired their own small plots of land on which they raised tobacco, and those who had no taste for agriculture migrated to Northern Rhodesia where they worked in the copper mines. The Nyasas were loyal to the Crown, and 60,000 of them fought in the First World War for Britain. Mission schools were good and numerous, and the Livingstone Mission encouraged boys to take an interest in the government of the country. Native associations, encouraged by the missions, were organized in the south and in the north and consulted with the colonial government on matters of native education and welfare, especially the welfare of Nyasas who went to the Rhodesias to work. Out of the Northern Association grew the Nyasaland African National Congress, the independence party, and it seemed in 1952 that the country was set for a peaceful transition to self-government.

In 1953, however, the British Conservative government federated Nyasaland with Northern and Southern Rhodesia and proclaimed its belief in an evolution of democratic institutions in partnership over the whole area.

This decision came as a great shock to the Nyasas and many of their white friends and leaders, like Dr. Hastings K. Banda (1902-   ), in voluntary exile in London. Nyasaland had very few white settlers—a few hundreds at most—and they and the missionaries never saw themselves except as helpers and advisers to the ninety-nine per cent of Nyasas. Northern Rhodesia had grown rich and had attracted 60,000 Europeans by 1953, most of them working in or with the copper mining industry. Although a 1930 Memorandum on Native Policy had established that there was to be no racial or religious discrimination in Northern Rhodesia, it was hard for the government in London to detect subtle forms of discrimination; and no government succeeded in ensuring equal pay for natives, even when they did the same work as whites in the mines. Native welfare associations multiplied, and grew into the Northern Rhodesian African National Congress, led by Harry Nkumbula (1916-   ), but few people took any notice of the associations. There was one white man to every forty Africans and this was a high enough proportion of whites to block most African political progress.

As far as the Nyasas were concerned, the situation in Southern Rhodesia was even worse. They were being asked to federate with a country whose 200,000 whites dominated the three million natives, with a monopoly of most of the social, political and economic institutions. A quarter of the land in Southern Rhodesia had been reserved for natives in 1920. In 1925, the Carter Report recommended that any empty lands should be quickly divided between the races to prevent any future squabbling, and the 1930 Land Apportionment Act did just this. After 1930, Europeans, mostly British, owned fifty-one per cent of the land, Africans thirty-one per cent, and the remainder was set aside for national parks and game preserves. Nobody seems to have protested against this allocation of land at the time, least of all the Rhodesian Labour Party which looked after white workers. The 1934 Industrial Conciliation Act, for which the

Labour Party was largely responsible, excluded Africans from wage bargaining.

During the thirties there had been some political activity in Southern Rhodesia by Africans. They had formed native associations to look after the welfare of workers in the mines, but many of the associations were more concerned with protecting their own members against the claims of immigrant natives than with claiming equal rights from the white man. In 1938, a Bantu Congress Party was formed, but this remained ineffectual until after the Second World War. White Rhodesians in the main supported the United Party, led by Godfrey Huggins (1883-   ) who ruled the self-governing colony virtually until the British government's decision to federate it with Northern Rhodesia and Nyasaland.

The proposal to federate the three territories, first made in 1951, was made in the belief that the three were natural partners. Nyasaland had too many people for her small acreage, and many of them already had experience working in the other two territories. Northern Rhodesia was one of the world's great sources of copper, and Southern Rhodesia had capital to invest as a result of successful, modern farming and the stable government which always attracts outside capital. Yet the Nyasas were not the only people to object to the proposal. Whites in Northern Rhodesia had proposed self-government for themselves in 1947, and their leader Roy Welensky (1907-   ) believed that Africans should remain under Colonial Office guidance. Whites in Southern Rhodesia, reading of plans for black majority rule in the Gold Coast, thought that federation was a subtle first step in that direction, and that the Nyasas and the Northern Rhodesian natives would swamp the federation's white population.

But in 1953 federation became a fact. The restricted number of electors (ninety-five per cent white) gave Southern Rhodesia, which had the largest white population, control of the Federal Assembly. There were twenty-four Southern Rhodesians, fourteen Northern Rhodesians, and six Nyasalanders, who made up the Assembly, after a revision of the constitution in 1957, and the whole was dominated by the indefatigable Huggins.

The danger of being swamped by the native population, should further revisions of the constitution give them a majority of voters, prompted the white Southern Rhodesians to reorganize their parties to strengthen them. The United Party was renamed the United Federal Party, and looked after white settlers' interests in the Federal Parliament, while a United Rhodesian Party, led by Garfield Todd (1908-   ), looked after their interests in the Southern Rhodesian Parliament. Sir Roy Welensky became Federal Prime Minister, guided by Huggins who became a peer as Lord Malvern. There was a liberal white opposition, the Confederate Party, whose place was taken in 1956 by the Dominion Party led by Winston Field (1904-   ). Field was in no way sympathetic to liberal causes in the European sense, and as fear of native political activity increased among the white settlers, his party posed a threat to United Rhodesian Party power in Southern Rhodesia. Todd, the Southern Rhodesian premier, was expelled from the United Rhodesian Party in 1957 for suggesting mild reforms which would have given the vote to more Africans, and Field strengthened his position still further.

In 1958 there was a general election in the Federation. The Congress parties, one for each territory, held meetings before the election and decided that federation had done nothing to look after African interests. The Congress leaders, Nkumbula, Kanyama, Chiume (1929-   ), and M. H. B. Chipembere (1931?-   ) decided to boycott the elections, and the Nyasas, Chiume and Chipembere sent for Dr. Hastings Banda, their nominal leader in exile in London. Banda was an experienced politician, who had learned his craft by studying the organizational methods of the British Labour Party. His return was the occasion for riots in Northern Rhodesia and Nyasaland, and Sir Roy Welensky, re-elected Federal Prime Minister, banned the territorial African Congress parties. Banda formed a Malawi Congress Party in Nyasaland, and his friend Kenneth Kaunda (1924-   ) formed a United National Independence Party in Northern Rhodesia. Both parties were pledged to fight for the dissolution of the Federation and independence for their territories.

Sir Roy Welensky and his friends, who had opposed the idea of federation in 1953, had had second thoughts. Under his administration a great deal of economic progress had been made in all three territories. The railway system had become one of the best in Africa, shipping out Northern Rhodesian copper and Southern Rhodesian agricultural products. An airline had also reached a peak of efficiency. These and other services were run by the federal government much more cheaply and efficiently than they had been run by the territorial governments. These services benefited white interests, of course, and co-operation between whites had been the only aspect of federation which had appealed to Welensky in 1953, but the general prosperity, especially of Southern Rhodesia, had benefited Africans, too. There was no doubt that housing conditions for Africans were better in Southern Rhodesia than in independent Ghana and Guinea, and hospital services incomparably better. Any dissolution of the federation would disrupt these federally-run services, and in any apportioning Southern Rhodesia would surely get the lion's share of men and institutions perfected during federation.

However, African opinion grew stronger day by day. After their boycott of the 1958 general election, leaders of the African parties organized a series of riots which confirmed the worst fears of those who believed that the road to independence for Africans was inevitably stained with blood. The federal government acted swiftly and banned all African parties. Dr. Hastings Banda reacted by declaring Nyasaland's independence unilaterally. He was promptly arrested and detained. Riots continued in Northern Rhodesia, though demonstrations were suppressed in the south. The British government set up an official inquiry, and in December 1960, there was a conference in London to review the whole question of federation. Inevitably, African representatives insisted on dissolution and independence with black majority rule, and when it was said that this was impracticable, they walked out of the conference. In 1961 there was a referendum on the future of the federation, and again Nyasaland and Northern Rhodesian African opinion was confirmed as hostile. In 1961, too, Nyasaland's first general election with an extended franchise made it clear that the Nyasas had had enough of the federation experiment, and wanted independence. In December 1962, the British government recognized Nyasaland's right to withdraw from the Federation and in March 1963, Northern Rhodesia, which had chosen its first African government on November 1, 1962, was given leave to withdraw. Discussions began to decide the date of elections which would prepare for full independence, granted to Nyasaland (as Malawi) on July 6, 1964, and to Northern Rhodesia (as Zambia) on October 24, 1964.

While Nyasaland and Zambia were hurrying down the road to independence with the approval of the British government, the settlers in Southern Rhodesia were digging in for a siege. They had no intention of extending the franchise and giving the Africans black majority rule. White refugees from Kenya, Uganda, Northern Rhodesia, and Nyasaland, even from former colonies in Asia, swelled the ranks of the "Rhodesia First" movement. The granting of independence to Algeria, a "brother settler state which owes all to Europeans" was the last straw which broke the liberals' back. In December 1962, Winston Field led his party (renamed the Rhodesian Front) to victory at the polls, and was succeeded in August 1964 as prime minister by Ian Smith (1919-   ). African parties led by Joshua Nkomo (1917-   ) (Zimbabwe African People's Union) and Rev. Ndabaningi Sithole (1920-   ) (Zimba African National Union), were banned and only the Zimbabwe National Party was allowed to exist legally.

Any attempt by white liberals in Southern Rhodesia (renamed simply Rhodesia) to suggest a widening of the franchise was received with a mixture of anger and amazement. Rhodesia was the only British "white man's country" left in Africa, and no change was possible in the foreseeable future.

African reaction to the Rhodesian stand was understandably bitter. In 1961 they had been offered a constitution which would have given Rhodesian Africans a majority of electors on the roll, though the voting system was such that a white government would have been elected. Nevertheless, white Rhodesian liberals felt at the time that it was a step forward, since it would at least train some Africans in government. Nkomo, leader of ZAPU, at first agreed to sign a memorandum approving the constitution, but later, under pressure from Nkrumah and other African leaders outside Rhodesia, he withdrew his support. During 1963 and 1964, seeing Malawi and Zambia attain their independence, Rhodesian Africans in the main became sullen and silent, many of their leaders seeking asylum with Banda or Kaunda. Africans outside Rhodesia continued to protest at the United Nations and at meetings of their own Organization of African Unity. But their protests were often uninformed. They accused white Rhodesians of racial discrimination on a par with that in South Africa, though it was far less in Rhodesia. Rhodesian Africans are as much entitled to use transport, hotels, and restaurants in Salisbury, as all whites—provided they have the money to pay. Discrimination does exist in wage scales, but there were by 1961 several very wealthy Africans, and many technicians earning high wages in industry.

The British Labour government, elected in the autumn of 1964, was sympathetic to the African Rhodesian cause. However, the British prime minister, Harold Wilson, tended to listen more to Africans outside Rhodesia than to those who could give a clear idea of their condition. White Rhodesians in Salisbury felt that this was ridiculous, that being badly informed about the situation, the British Labour government would rush Rhodesia towards black majority rule as soon as they could find a way to do so. On November 11, 1965, the Rhodesian premier, Ian Smith, unilaterally declared Rhodesia independent. It was an illegal act, as complete independence could only be granted to a self-governing colony like Rhodesia after agreement with the British government, and the British government wanted "guarantees of African progress." Nevertheless, since November 1965, Rhodesia has been effectively independent—as a British "white man's country," and attempts to defeat the illegal regime have failed. It is probably true that when a nation state makes up its mind that it wants independence, no legal power in the world can prevent it from gaining it.

13 *New Nations of Africa; achievements and promise*

SINCE THEY GAINED THEIR INDEPENDENCE, THE NEW nations of Africa, whatever the language of the imperial power they once served, have followed a curiously similar path of political, social and economic progress.

Relations with the former imperial power quickly became amicable. After all, once independence had been achieved, there was really little to quarrel about. Ties between former colonial subjects of France and Paris, and between former colonial subjects of Great Britain and London, remained strong, as was to be expected. Most of the African leaders have been educated in Paris or London, and speak English or French as well as they speak their tribal languages. In many cases, de-tribalized Africans have more in common with men from other tribes who speak their European language than they have with their own tribesmen.

The imperial powers themselves have shown some anxiety to establish good relations with Africans who were, until a few years ago, their enemies, often jailed for subversive activities. There are many Englishmen and Frenchmen genuinely eager to help the new nations to achieve political stability and economic prosperity. After all, the British Fabian Society gave direction to the first independence movements. There are also Englishmen and Frenchmen anxious to help the governments of the new states because they are afraid that Communist help will be forthcoming if they do not.

In the field of international relations, it is interesting to note that few African states have established close ties with Communist countries. Sékou Touré turned to the Soviet Union and China for help when he was virtually blockaded by the French in 1958, and for a while it seemed that Conakry, the capital of Guinea, was going to become a Communist base in Africa. However, three years later, Sékou Touré expelled the Soviet ambassador because Communist aid seemed to have too many strings attached to it—Communist diplomats were preaching politics instead of giving the technical aid and advice they had offered. Similarly, the government of the Congo expelled the whole Soviet delegation in 1961, when it found the delegation profiting by the internal disorders to preach still more revolution.

Most African states try to maintain good relations with both Communist and non-Communist countries, with both Arabs and Jews, with both Indians and Pakistanis. Foreigners' quarrels are no business of Africa, which needs all the aid and advice it can get, and a great deal of capital to build up industry and modernize agriculture. Roman Catholics like the president of Tanzania (Tanganyika and Zanzibar) are on good terms with their opposite numbers in Moscow and Peking. Left-wing African leaders like Sékou Touré of Guinea get along well with right-wing politicians in Europe, even with General de Gaulle. Africans are not anxious to join the West or the East. Having fought for their independence, they refuse to lose it again, even in return for badly-needed trade and aid.

In the field of internal relations, between states inside Africa, the new states have often disappointed each other. In a sense they compete with each other, for foreign aid and attention, so cannot be very good friends. Yet they have many interests in common, and have set up bodies like the Organization of African Unity which are supposed to stress these common interests. There are, however, many difficulties. Some African leaders speak English, others French. There are so many tribal languages that without these two languages, little communication of any sort would be possible; but even with the limiting of the number of languages used to two, there is still a lack of understanding. Everything said or written has to be translated, and meetings can only be held where there are translation facilities. Francophile Africans often have ideas about government which are unrecognizable to their Anglophile friends. Political institutions tend to be as different as national diets. There are also religious barriers. Muslim African states are still suspicious of Christianity as the white man's religion, though many African leaders are Christians.

Nevertheless, inside the different states the same sort of problems have been faced. A tiny minority of the population in each state is politically educated. The detribalized members of the government have little in common with men and women still living tribally. Tribal chiefs who took orders reluctantly from white men often refuse to be ordered about by men who are renegades from the tribe. For the future, all states need a vast program of political education if the tribes are to understand something of the complicated workings of a modern state and economy. For the short term, the temptation has been to weaken the opposition by imprisoning its leaders. In most African states there is only one party. Opposition parties have been banned because they would "disrupt the state." In some cases, the different parties have joined together—as in Guinea—and a one-party state has been created voluntarily, because there are so few competent politicians that more than one party is a luxury they cannot afford.

A more disturbing development in Africa has been the suppression of what little democracy exists in a one-party state. The party in power has slowly become more and more corrupt. Personal enemies of the leader of the party have been jailed for no apparent reason. Censorship of the press has followed, with the expulsion of foreign journalists who criticized what was happening to freedom in these countries. Foreign aid and native capital have been used to build palaces and prestige buildings, and little by little the atmosphere of a dictatorship has become heavy enough almost to stifle dreams of freedom. In many cases, Africans are less free than they were under colonial rule.

Mr. R. T. Paget, writing in the London *Daily Telegraph,* suggested in 1966 that African governments (like all other governments) should be judged on their performance.

"What are they doing to broaden their base, to increase admission to the educated minority? What are they doing to develop their country? What are they doing to bridge the economic gap between the rulers and the ruled? How near do they get to honesty? . . . Is law and order maintained? How many enemies does the Government have to keep in gaol? Is administration reasonably humane?"

Recently, Africans have reacted against the corruption of the one-party state and there have been a series of military coups d'état. Even leaders of independence movements like Nkrumah of Ghana and Balewa of Nigeria have been dethroned, and military governments have taken their place. Seven African governments have fallen to the leaders of their armies, who have announced a drive to clean up the state and prepare for a return to a real democracy. Other African governments are dependent on their armies for survival.

The principal difficulty African states have found is that of establishing an "African way of life." Africans educated abroad want to live in houses or apartments with proper sanitation, go to schools and universities, own automobiles and wear European clothes. There are, however, millions of Africans who still live in straw-roofed huts, wear a single piece of cloth wrapped around their bodies, and never see a school. Tribal chiefs often discourage attempts to modernize their people, believing that once educated and with money of their own, they will refuse to obey the chiefs. Governments are not very enthusiastic about the idea of dethroning the chiefs, because they have no system of local government and justice to put in the place of the original, traditional one. And so there are in fact two Africas—the Africa of the cities, with modern buildings and a European way of life, and the Africa of the villages, with mud huts, meals of rice and roots and customs of their own. The new Africa has control of most of the wealth and the power, but it cannot exist without, or ignore, the old Africa.

Africa's future will be clear only when Africans come to terms with their own past and the world's present and future.

CHRONOLOGICAL TABLE

B.C. 11000   Ancestors of Bushmen in Sudan; Hamites in East Africa
  3000   Ancient Egyptians come to Nile Valley
  2000   First Pyramids
  1300   Rameses II rules in Egypt; Moses born a few years later
   610   King Necho of Egypt attempts to dig a Suez Canal
   525   Persian invasion of Egypt
   332   Alexander invades Egypt
   146   Roman conquest of Egypt and North Africa; Roman settlers in what is now Tunisia
A.D. 30   Christianity first penetrates Egypt
    60   Roman Emperor Nero sends expedition to discover source of the Nile
   180   Christianity arrives in North Africa
   428   Vandals invade North Africa
   640   Islam brought to Africa by Arab traders and missionaries
   650   Kingdom of Songhai in West Africa founded by Berbers
   770   Ghana conquered by Negroes
  1050   Muslim invasion of West Africa
  1250   Mali Empire established in West Africa; first evidence of stable settlement in Shona (now Rhodesia)
  1300   Mansa Musa the Magnificent rules over Mali
  1415   Prince Henry of Portugal encourages exploration of African coasts; Chinese fleet arrives off Somalia
  1446   Beginning of Portuguese slave trade
  1490   First missionaries in the Congo
  1500   Kingdoms of Buganda, Toro, Bunyoro and Busoga in East Africa
  1590   British, French, Dutch and Prussians establish trading stations on West African coast
  1652   First Dutch settlement at the Cape in South Africa
  1787   British anti-slavers found Sierra Leone as home for ex-slaves
  1818   Zulus massacre neighboring tribes in South Africa
  1822   Liberia founded by American Colonization Society
  1830   Algeria conquered by French
  1835   Boers begin the Great Trek
  1838   Boer republics founded in Transvaal
  1844   German exploration in East Africa; Livingstone's expedition
  1854   French expansion in West Africa
  1869   Opening of Suez Canal

1880
-1 First Boer War
1884 Berlin Conference convenes to settle details of partition of Africa between imperial powers
1899 Second Boer War begins
1902 Peace of Vereeniging signals end of second Boer War
1910 Union of South Africa established

1919 Germany's African territories ceded to Britain and South Africa by League of Nations mandate
1922 Self-government in Egypt
1923 Self-government in Rhodesia
1931 British Commonwealth established; South Africa independent
1935 Italy invades Ethiopia
1939- Gradual disintegration of Old French Empire
45   •
1956 French grant limited self-government to colonies
1957 Independence of Gold Coast as Ghana
1958 French Community formed; Guinea refuses to join and becomes independent
1960 French Community collapses; independence granted to Togo, Cameroon, Mali, Senegal, Madagascar, Somalia, Dahomey, Niger, Upper Volta, Ivory Coast, Chad, Central African Republic, Gabon, Mauritania and French Congo; independence of Belgian Congo and of Nigeria
1961 Independence of Sierra Leone and Tanganyika; South Africa leaves British Commonwealth
1962 Independence of Algeria, Burundi, Rwanda and Uganda
1963 Independence of Kenya; Zanzibar becomes independent, joins Tanganyika to form Tanzania
1964 Independence of Nyasaland as Malawi and of Northern Rhodesia as Zambia
1965 Independence of Gambia; Rhodesia declares herself independent
1966 Independence of Basutoland as Lesotho and of Bechuanaland as Botswana

INDEX

186

DATE DUE

DATE DUE			
FEB 25 '72			
APR 15 '86			
JUN 14 '88			
FEB 24 '90			
GAYLORD			PRINTED IN U.S.A.